READING AND WRITING THE SELF

Autobiography in Education and the Curriculum

Robert J. Graham

TEACHERS COLLEGE PRESS

Teachers College, Columbia University
New York and London

Published by Teachers College Press, 1234 Amsterdam Avenue
New York, NY 10027

Library of Congress Cataloging-in-Publication Data

Graham, Robert J., 1941–
    Reading and writing the self : autobiography in education and the
curriculum / Robert J. Graham.
        p.   cm. — (Critical issues in curriculum)
    Revision of the author's thesis (doctoral—University of Calgary).
    Includes bibliographical references (p.) and index.
    ISBN 0–8077–3126–9 (alk. paper) — ISBN 0–8077–3125–0 (pbk.
alk. paper)
    1. Autobiography.   2. English language—Composition and exercises—
Study and teaching.   3. Self-realization.   4. Self in literature.
5. Curriculum planning.   I. Title.   II. Series.
LB1576.G725   1991
808′.042′07—dc20   91–28495
                                                                    CIP

ISBN 0–8077–3126–9
ISBN 0–8077–3125–0 (pbk.)

Printed on acid-free paper
Manufactured in the United States of America

98 97 96 95 94 93 92 91   8 7 6 5 4 3 2 1

Contents

Foreword

This book marks the launching of a new series, **Critical Issues in Curriculum.** Robert Graham's thorough and accomplished analysis of autobiography as a way of knowing offers an auspicious opening for the series. Graham's book, like those that will follow, encourages readers to come to grips with an innovative idea that inspires new programs and raises serious challenges to old ones. Although the use of autobiography takes a number of forms, from grade school to graduate school, its modest but not insubstantial pedagogical goal is "to bridge the gap," as Graham puts it succinctly in the first chapter, "between a knower and an object of knowledge." *Only connect*, one might say of autobiography's educational theme. The autobiographical turn directs learning inward, to one's own story, as if to follow the Socratic adage, "Know thyself." As Graham makes vividly clear in his descriptions of programs inspired by this sensibility, students are asked to respond to literature out of their own experience; to lay out the pattern of their own lives in composition class; to reflect on the day's lessons in a diary of their learning. The pursuit of self-knowledge encourages students to find themselves in the classroom, perhaps for the first time. It proves no less a force in inspiring those teachers returning to graduate school who are asked to take hold of their own teaching by tracing out its narrative line through their own writing. Education is, after all, a chapter in everyone's tale, and for the teacher the chapter gradually forms a life in the classroom.

Yet whether or not the enthusiastic use of autobiography by these educators amounts to a new manner of thinking about curriculum, Graham finds the conception at this point only partially thought out. He carefully lays out the underlying assumptions about learning, self, and text that mark this quest for the "authentic voice" of experience in the classroom. In the course of this inquiry, Graham unearths its impetus in John Dewey's influential celebration of children's experience; he traces the transatlantic variations in its realization; and he deftly brings advances in literary theory to bear on education's conception of what is, in the first instance, a genre, a particular form of text. The book's considerable educational scope and intellectual range, its feeling for classrooms, and its command of interdisciplinary perspectives, are no less than is required to make sense of this issue in curriculum. Yet for all of that, it can be said that Graham wears his scholarship lightly and with grace as he lucidly and cogently presents the consequences of this autobiographical urge in education.

Graham's book, in a feature intended to mark this new series, is written to reach a wide audience of those concerned with education. It is scholarship committed to advancing the understanding and practice of innovative curriculum measures. Yet it must be said that the book speaks wonderfully well for itself; it is his story in that sense, and I could do no better than to leave it at that. With his permission, however, I would add a few more words on the intent of the new series to provide a further context for his work and the books to come.

To begin with, there is a double sense to the term *critical* in this series title. Timeliness is certainly one aspect. As with Graham's book, it seems far better to catch these developments on the rise, to inform educators about what is at stake, but also to give pause to those caught up in the middle of the issue. That is, these timely books will also have a critical edge to them. They will raise disconcerting questions that tend to get overlooked amid the headlong enthusiasm of advocates and participants; they will offer educators the benefit of the relevant educational research on an international scale. The books will hold to what is lived and sensed by teachers and students caught in the midst of these changes and issues. The series will, at times, deal with specific school programs of study, going after the nitty-gritty of what is taught and tested. At other times, it will track how aspects of the curriculum permeate not only all that student and teacher experience (the taught and the caught), but also the way in which the curriculum signifies what is hidden within, as well as what is excluded from, the classroom. The first critical lesson of the series is not a new one—the curriculum is the medium and the medium is the message.

As timely as these critical issues are, many of them take their sense of urgency from an earlier promise, first made when public schooling became part of the argument for the extension of democracy in the nineteenth century. Since then, the schools have opened their doors, if not always readily, to the political curriculum of civil rights, equality of opportunity, religious freedom, and gender equity; they have also become the playground of tax revolt, censorship fights, and other less encouraging measures. The schools have responded to this heady traffic in waves of educational reform. It is always a matter of trying to do the right thing in the classroom, to get more from the chalkboard hours spent between the morning bell and the bus ride home. Yet this dedication and sincerity in the curriculum want for a theme of constancy. Some educators are always on the lookout for what seems bright and engaging; others hold fast to the certain stability of what worked last year. All of them are wrestling with the Kafkaesque levels of educational governance. It can make for an uncertain experience, with both daring and staid teachers nagged by questions about the adequacy of their choices, and students wending their way through the curricular spectrum.

It is in light of this situation that **Critical Issues in Curriculum** proposes to apply a steady eye and a firm hand to what is urgent and timely, as well as pressing and promising, in the way that schools organize learning. Beginning with Graham's book on autobiography in education, the series will pursue the impact of new program initiatives, school reorganization drives, and cultural and political movements. In this, the series seeks a renewal of the field of curriculum studies by renouncing the excesses of door-to-door consultants and critics, scholars and saviors. The books published in this series will treat educational issues with a sense of urgency and concern that amounts to a committed scholarship. They will not have all of the answers, but they will seek new sources of insight and take up the relevant questions frankly and with feeling; they will reflect the lessons gained from prior efforts; and they will proceed as if the way forward really began with the articulation of possibility.

It is a series designed to meet the needs of this post-it age of postmodernism, poststructuralism, and postcolonialism given to its air of intellectual excitement, its sense of *getting beyond*. The postmodern is rife with eclecticism, selectively appropriating and questioning the usable past that in itself forms one way of getting beyond its tyranny. Not so much the new, but the renewed and reworked, and as with an eye on the past, the over-the-shoulder look. Such is the contemporary and self-conscious curriculum that this series takes up, supports, and challenges, in its eternal revision. Already the humanities are being rewritten; the classics of Western Civilization are taking on a becoming humility amid newly discovered realms of expression. Plato meets Zora Neale Hurston, and the simple matter of selecting a text, as the curriculum's principal artifact, becomes an enormously critical issue. The curriculum is no longer learning's tidy house. Every step in the making of the curriculum becomes its own lesson.

There is, however, more to the curriculum of postmodernity than affixing warning labels to the classics. Not all of the changes are so hotly contested as the supplanting and supplementing of the classics. With less commotion and benefits spreading across the curriculum, there is a new emphasis on writing as a way of learning and on historical inquiry as a way of contextualizing knowledge. Not only are the disciplines examined for what they make of the world, but attention is now turned on the child's construction of knowledge and understanding. New questions are being asked about the very nature of text and author, about what counts as knowledge and interpretation. What have been assumed to be the central concerns of curriculum—ideals of teaching and learning, skills and abilities, imagination and creativity, intelligence and achievement—have lost their easy innocence and assumed essence. We can no longer proceed as if we were certain of these terms' timeless meanings. They are, in fact, fabricated at the meeting-place of culture and history, and as such they must be read for what they embrace and exclude, for what they make of the classroom, child, and teacher. In this, the series will treat the curriculum as a test-site for the theories by which we live, for who we would be. Sometimes the schoolhouse is our best story, with all that implies, and sometimes not.

Certainly, the resurgence of interest in what teachers bring to the front of the classroom has led to talk in highly visible political forums of national and core curriculums, of centralized testing and international comparative studies of achievement, and of revamping teacher education and evaluation. For many, education has become a matter of ensuring economic viability served up in a rhetoric of national renewal that can resemble a looping shuttle bus, constantly picking up new passengers with each stop. But that's only part of the current educational story. From somewhat closer to the chalkface, and to the heart of Graham's book, a number of educators have thrown their support behind classroom reforms that draw on a different agenda. Most notable, perhaps, is the growing number of teachers involved in the development of whole language programs, supporting their work through networks and the semiofficial National Writing Project. Others are introducing integrated programs of study that attempt to break down the fragmentation curriculum. Still others are beginning to initiate innovative approaches based on new, vitally important understandings of gender and culture in educational settings. Certainly, curriculum is at the forefront of the fight to foster schools that make a positive difference in the lives of the young and thus the future of the nation. Curriculum itself has become a critical and contested focal point, perhaps *the* point when it comes to the life of a child sitting at a desk, pencil poised, at the beginning of any school day. Whatever winds come to buffet or refresh the schools, the curriculum cannot help but be moved, sometimes with renewed promises, sometimes with old ones deferred.

With Graham's *Reading and Writing the Self*, **Critical Issues in Curriculum** begins to explore an important aspect of the time that students and teachers spend together, in what they come to make of themselves. The ideas nurtured here suggest that it is indeed always possible to foster what is fascinating, encouraging, and productive; to find a greater part of the promise that drives the educational commitment of so many. Students and teachers deserve nothing less, and here follows an insightful book that has more than its share to offer.

John Willinsky

Acknowledgments

This book began life as a doctoral thesis undertaken in the Department of Curriculum and Instruction at the University of Calgary. Consequently, my greatest debt must be reserved for John Willinsky, who as supervisor, mentor, and friend believed in and understood the nature of the project better than I did, and prodded, cajoled, and provoked as it lurched toward completion. I count myself fortunate indeed to have kept such company on that particular journey, and I take great pleasure in being able to publicly thank John and his wife, Pam, for their many kindnesses.

I incurred many debts both intellectual and personal before and during the various stages of preparing the book for publication. Many years ago Kathryn Chittick challenged me to challenge myself, and for this and her constant interest in my work, I thank her. I also want to thank Douglas A. Roberts, from whose wise counsel and great practicality I benefited on several occasions. Thanks also to Anne McWhir and William Hunter who, as members of the thesis committee, offered many helpful suggestions. Kieran Egan acted as external reader, and his comments invariably forced me to reconsider some of my more fanciful flights. Garth Benson was always there with books to lend and was never too busy to let me regale him with whatever ideas were exciting me at the time. I benefited greatly from Pamela McCallum's course on literary theory, and, in a less formal situation, from my talks with Linda Brandau.

Helen Harper, LaDonna Macrae, Muriel Hamilton, Elizabeth Sparks, Carolle Debert, Helen Christansen, and Carmen Maier all, at one time or another, lent their encouragement and support. My thanks, too, to Roger Woock, now of the University of Melbourne, for providing strong coffee, cigars, and a stimulating forum for debate. Likewise, I am also grateful to Margaret Hunsburger, whose idea for a "brown bag" seminar compelled me to crystallize many of the book's central points of view at a crucial time.

I am pleased to acknowledge here the kindness of William Pinar, who read an entire draft of the manuscript and circulated chapters on my behalf. I hope the book repays in some small measure these unbidden acts of generosity. Similarly, William Schubert made some very encouraging observations and remarks at a time when these were greatly appreciated. Richard Butt, generous to a fault, sent draft copies of his work and traded personal stories with me on several memorable occasions. Wendy Strachan sent articles, books, and good cheer, while Stanley Straw has proved an unfailing source of friendship, conversation, and sound advice. Thanks also to John Seymour, a department head never too busy to listen, and a man of understanding in times of stress.

During the writing of the thesis I was the recipient of a Social Sciences and Research Council of Canada Doctoral Fellowship, without which completing this work would have proved a more difficult task. I take pleasure in acknowledging their assistance. Chapter 2 appeared in slightly different form in the *Journal of Educational Thought*, and I am grateful to the editors for permission to republish it here. Brian Ellerbeck of Teachers College Press has been a source of stimulation and critical insight and Karl Nyberg has seen the book through its various stages with great conscientiousness. My thanks also go to Pamela LaBarbiera, whose copyediting saved me from an embarrassing number of stylistic errors. Those that remain are entirely my own responsibility.

Finally, my wife, Lori Downey, has provided unfailing and selfless support throughout the entire process. Fittingly enough, our daughter, Rachel, was born as the book neared completion, and I therefore dedicate this book to Lori and Rachel with my love.

READING AND WRITING THE SELF

Autobiography in Education and the Curriculum

1 Discovering Autobiography in Education

Somebody was in my office the other day asking me to write my auto-biography. What I couldn't tell them was that everything I write I consider autobiography although nobody else would.

Northrop Frye, 1988

The success of the word "autobiography" is undoubtedly linked to the ambiguity or the indecisiveness that it permits, to the new space of reading and interpretation that it makes possible, to the new strategies of writing that it can designate. And this is even more evident with the adjective "autobiographical," which is certainly used as much as the substantive.

Philippe Lejeune, 1989

One of the permanent legacies bequeathed to the field of education by the work of conceptual analysts such as Hirst (1974), Peters (1966), and Scheffler (1975) has been to show how the most common terms used in educational talk and writing, terms like "teaching," "learning," or "the curriculum," are often the most misunderstood, simply because they are the most familiar and taken for granted. These writers' analyses have assisted greatly in establishing education on a firmer philosophical foundation, a foundation on which educators can build with more assurance and understanding. If concepts like teaching and learning are fundamental to any discourse on education, then just as surely investigations into these concepts have moved quickly beyond common-sense notions to uncover other unspoken and tacit dimensions. As this study will show in detail, the same holds true for the analysis of the place of autobiography in education and the curriculum. Consequently, as a thread that will run

1

through all subsequent discussions, I will argue that a clearer understanding of autobiography will make a significant contribution toward setting the external boundaries of curricular knowledge, as well
as helping to define "what constitutes valid sources of information
from which come accepted theories, principles, and ideas relevant to
the field of curriculum" (Ornstein & Hunkins, 1988, p. 9).

At first glance, autobiography and the autobiographical would
seem unlikely candidates for making significant contributions to our
knowledge of education and the curriculum. In some ways it would
surely make more sense to view autobiography as a genre of some
interest to literary scholars, rather than one of importance to educators. Nevertheless, the writing of autobiography, as well as other
autobiographical discourses such as letters, journals, and diaries that
can be included in the "autobiographical pact" (Lejeune, 1989, p. 3)
between a writer and an audience, can be discovered functioning in a
number of important sites and initiatives within education. As a result, it will be one of this book's central purposes to show that, although an increasing number of educators are already employing
autobiography in their programs in greater and lesser degrees of sophistication, it exists as yet in the mind of the educational community
at large in an *undertheorized* state. It is this situation that militates
against a widespread consciousness and appreciation of its importance and that this book will remedy in a number of interconnected
ways. In addition, although autobiography and autobiographical discourses are being employed intuitively by some educators as both
process and product, as an element in a text and as a text in itself its
protean nature often makes it difficult to gain any clear sense of the
kinds of specific claims that are being made on its behalf. This book
will provide not only a map of some educational territory where the
use of autobiography has begun to alter the contours of practice, but
will also provide a theoretical compass (see Chapters 2 and 3) as an
orienting device for the journey.

And yet it should be said at once that many fields of inquiry
within education are not all agreed or seem to be talking about the
same phenomenon when they mention their reliance on autobiography or on the autobiographical. In spite of this, I maintain that far
from rendering the concept slippery and unattainable, these disagreements conceal the source of its power and of its claim on our
attention. This source is to be found precisely in its capacity not only
to enclose within itself—and to cause us to become engaged with—
principles and ideas of broadest concern to a wide range of educators,
but also in its ability to keep these ideas constantly in play, constantly

combining and recombining themselves in provocative new ways. Some ideas and elements that immediately spring to mind and that will receive more comprehensive treatment later are: conceptions of knowledge and the forms of knowledge; theories of the self, of personality, and of identity; psychological ideas of development; theories of language and learning; and finally, though by no means exhausting the possibilities, the problems involved in the use of autobiography as an instrument of research.

From this selective list, it is clear that to theorize more adequately the current status of autobiography will not only open up fresh avenues for inquiry within education (by clarifying further our understanding of what the concept itself entails), but that by "raising to explicit, reflective consciousness that which is already implicitly grasped" (Earle, 1977, p. 10), we will begin to understand the existential bases that make knowing possible.

The remainder of this first chapter will be concerned with discussing what might be involved in warranting the kinds of claims required to sustain these arguments. As well, an important part of this chapter will provide a cursory inspection of specific sites of inquiry where autobiography presently does the work of informing and guiding a number of important educational projects. For the present, however, a logical place to begin is to consider briefly some initial epistemological issues, since whether autobiography is used in language arts in order to write the self (Britton, 1970a), or methodologically in teacher education courses (Abbs, 1976, 1979; Grumet, 1981), or in reconceptualizing curriculum studies (Pinar, 1975; Pinar & Grumet, 1976), in each instance certain claims are being made for it as a way of gaining knowledge. However, it is not my primary objective here to make teachers feel more at ease about using autobiography at the level of school program by improving the quality of their practical arguments (Fenstermacher, 1986), although that may turn out to be an incidental by-product of what follows; rather, I want to explore the proposition that to talk at all about knowledge and the curriculum is inevitably to talk about the self and the manner in which that self makes the flux of experience intelligible. It is in effect to talk about education in its largest sense, whether one conceives education as a developmental process of unfolding or growth, or as an initiation into worthwhile activities. For if all knowledge begins in self-knowledge, or is a function of self-knowledge, then we cannot be said to truly know something until we have possessed it, made it our own.

Interestingly, then, autobiography stands in direct relation to traditional theories of knowledge that represent the tension between rationalist and pragmatist positions. In this respect Paul Hirst's work might be said to contain the most influential rationalist theory of knowledge and the curriculum, while John Dewey's instrumental theory sees knowledge as an active and exploratory process in which the conceptual instruments of thought are human constructions. The point to remember here is that, although Hirst's philosophical account provides a logical basis for education (that is, it can tell us *what* students could learn in terms of the forms of knowledge that one might wish to include in the curriculum), it contains neither a fully articulated account of who the recipients of this knowledge are in terms of gender, race, or class, nor of the social and institutional aspects involved in the construction of that knowledge. On the other hand, Dewey's account deals not only with the what and the how, but with *who* it is that is doing the learning. In other words, it provides a logical, psychological, and social view of knowledge creation that emphasizes its situated, relational, active, and experiential nature. For these reasons I will now briefly engage Hirst's and Dewey's views, not only as they pertain to the curriculum, but as they pertain to students situated in classrooms as institutional sites given over to the creation and the appropriation of meaning.

I want to argue first that autobiography, far from being a fuzzy, romantic concept with only a marginal claim on our attention, is a legitimate field of knowledge whose inclusion in the curriculum can be defended on strictly rational grounds. But second, even if this rational justification is persuasive for educators, we need to see autobiography at work in a number of fully-developed contexts within education and the curriculum in order to appreciate both the problems and the potential associated with its use. The major task of providing an exposition and discussion of these contexts will occupy much of our attention as we spend time surveying some specific educational sites in Chapters 3 through 6 below.

AUTOBIOGRAPHY AND THE FORMS OF KNOWLEDGE

One of the strongest claims Hirst (1974) makes in his widely discussed theorizing of the seven forms of knowledge (the empirical, the moral, the aesthetic, the mathematical, the philosophical, the religious, and the historical/sociological) concerns the role he believes they can play as an arbitrator of the curriculum: They are able to tell us what subjects to include and what to leave out. This aspect of curricular deduction is important for teachers and workers in curriculum since it seems to provide a strongly rational basis for making difficult practical choices about the shape of the curriculum itself. However, Hirst's views have been variously interpreted as supporting a subject-centered over a child-centered conception of education, and hence of rationalizing an elitist school system (Brent, 1978; White, 1973). It is beyond the framework of this chapter to enter into the intricacies of that debate; suffice it to say that Hirst's theory will be outlined here in order to allow us to approach the topic of autobiography from an unusual angle. Specifically, this angle will consist of disclosing the rational grounds for using autobiography at the level of school program, whether mandated by subject guidelines like language arts, social studies, or health education, or whether employed methodologically by instructors in universities as a way of having students reflect on their educational experiences. Consequently, there will be no detailed recapitulation of Hirst's argument and spirited defense of the forms of knowledge as such (Hirst, 1974); rather, Hirst's main claims will be employed instrumentally to support the general argument for a new appreciation of the place autobiography might be made to occupy in the curriculum.

As Brent (1978) makes clear in his critique of Hirst's position, the forms of knowledge do not exist "in some metaphysical realm that is both unverifiable and indescribable" (p. 94), but in a public language where they are not only capable of being described, but are "linguistically analysable by those who use them" (p. 95). Here we might remind ourselves again that Hirst identifies seven forms of knowledge: the empirical, the mathematical, the philosophical, the moral, the aesthetic, the religious, and the historical/sociological. In summary, the forms can be distinguished as follows (Hirst, 1974, p. 44):

1. Each form involves certain central concepts that are peculiar in character to the form, for example, gravity, number.
2. In a given form, these concepts form a network of possible relationships, that is, the form has a distinctive, logical structure.
3. By virtue of this logic, the form has expressions or statements that are testable against experience in accordance with criteria peculiar to the form.
4. The forms have developed particular techniques for testing their distinctive expressions, for example, scientific techniques or interpretive techniques.

But it might be asked, why are there no more than seven forms of knowledge, and why these particular ones? Hirst's reply is that we can apply irreducibility criteria to any of the forms. Hirst wants us to bear in mind that any subject (for example, language arts) is seen to best advantage via the activities commonly associated with "doing" that subject. In the instance of language arts, however, representative activities—such as judging characters' choices in a novel, discussing feelings aroused by a poem, or reading a short story set in another time—fail an irreducibility criterion. They fail it by being themselves reducible to the various forms of knowledge. However, if we go on to inspect the forms of knowledge themselves, we discover that the forms so engaged by these typical activities are not reducible either to one another, or to "any further all-embracing form of knowledge" (Brent, 1978, p. 97).

In addition to demonstrating the difference between a form of knowledge and a subject, Hirst shows that the forms of knowledge contain certain kinds of concepts or categories, as well as other non-categorial concepts that, following Brent (1978), will be called "substantive concepts" (p. 101). For example, in the empirical form of knowledge alluded to above, categorial concepts might include space and time, whereas substantive concepts might include atom and electron. What this implies for our example of language arts is that there are categorial concepts peculiar to the various forms of knowledge that are embodied in activities typically associated with that subject. Here categorial concepts associated with the moral form of knowledge used to judge a character's choices in a novel would involve considerations of right and wrong, while substantive concepts involved in reading a short story set in a different time period might involve considerations of class or gender. However, one must guard against equating Hirst's conceptions of the forms of knowledge with traditional curricular subjects. To do so would be to embrace a peculiarly closed view of knowledge, and indeed to lend support to the notion of building a curriculum around the traditional subject areas. What needs to be stressed is that the forms of knowledge can be discovered to a greater or lesser degree in all subjects. One need only think here of the moral and aesthetic aspects of doing science. For as Hirst (1974) himself notes, "School subjects . . . are in no way sacrosanct on either logical or psychological grounds. They are necessarily selections from the forms of knowledge that we have and may or may not be good as introductions for the purposes of liberal education" (p. 50).

The real point here is to view certain subjects as paradigmatic of the forms, so that a subject like language arts exemplifies in a powerful way the moral, aesthetic, and historical forms that it embodies but with which it is not identical. If we bear this in mind, then we can see that in this view of knowledge new subjects (or as Hirst calls them, fields of knowledge) can be generated out of the forms in various ways. Thus it can be argued that just as physics would seem more satisfactory as an exemplar of scientific thinking, autobiography itself can stand as the exemplar of another equally valuable and irreducible way of thinking and knowing. It is apparent, then, that engaging in the moral, aesthetic, and historical forms of knowledge discovered in autobiography will immerse the student in the operating principles, values, and truth-criteria that are involved in the way of knowing activated by the use of narrative. In this respect narrative represents the cognitive functioning described by Bruner (1986) as a "mode of thought" (p. 11), a mode whose truth is discovered in verisimilitude and not in appeals to procedures "for establishing formal and empirical proof" (p. 11).

Although I have taken into account writing and speaking activities, I have failed to account for what many language arts teachers feel are activities of equal importance, namely reading and interpretation. Indeed Hirst (1974) himself, in his observations on the role of subject disciplines in his blueprint for the curriculum, states that not only must students become immersed in the concepts, logic, and criteria of the discipline, but that they must cover "the whole range of the discipline so that [their] experience begins to be widely structured in this distinctive manner" (p. 47). In other words, it is necessary to examine the so-called passive or receptive aspects of language arts (reading, listening) as well as its more obvious active aspects (writing, speaking). Therefore, how can we say that the activities of reading and interpreting themselves are somehow autobiographical in the manner suggested here? A detailed answer to this question cannot detain us long, but a sketch of an answer can be given that will at least point toward the direction we might begin to look.

The rudiments of an answer are to be found in the influential views of literary theorists Stanley Fish (1980), Norman Holland (1980), and Louise Rosenblatt (1969, 1978), critics concerned with theories of "reader-response." Briefly, Fish's argument issues from his reservations over the reading methods of New Criticism, especially its minimizing of the reader's role and the championing of Wimsatt and Beardsley's (1954) "affective fallacy," the principle that stated that the meaning of a text should not be confused with the states of emotion it calls forth in a reader. It is precisely this affective element that Fish wants to reinstate, since to do so would relocate the locus of meaning in the experience of a reader rather than in the text. For Fish (1980), a sentence is an event, "something that *happens* to, and with the participation of the reader" (p. 125, emphasis in original). Because of this, interpretation is "an analysis of the developing response of the reader in relation to the words as they succeed one another in time" (pp. 126–127). This view of interpretation is what Freund (1987) calls "the drama of cognitive mediation taking place in the encounter of text and mind" (p. 93). We can begin to see here that interpretation from a reader-response perspective is indeed an active, cognitive, constructive process, one in which the emotions stirred up by the text are not only welcomed, but in fact encouraged, as a reader monitors these shifting states of consciousness. Not only can there be no meaning without a reader, but the meaning resides in the reader's experience, all of it, states of emotion included. In other words, we as readers are active, we "'write' the texts we read" (Freund, 1987, p. 153) by using the cognitive capacities of our minds.

On the other hand, Norman Holland's psychoanalytic approach to reader-response criticism, what he calls "transactive criticism," sees readers using the literary text to re-create themselves, their own identities. As Holland (1980) has constantly maintained, "interpretation is a function of identity" (p. 123), that is, as an individual is, so does he or she read. The manner in which we respond to a text is determined by our identity theme, a view of the self that Holland, as committed ego psychologist, sees as a continuing and unchanging core to our personalities. Holland has coined the acronym DEFT (defenses, expectations, fantasies, and transformations) to describe the process by which our experience is adapted and assimilated into the ego. This individual style of coping with the world is replicated in the particular style of the interpretation.

Finally, Louise Rosenblatt (1978) centers the interpretive act firmly in the temporally developing responses of the reader. In her distinction between efferent and aesthetic reading, she maintains that an encounter with a literary text is best considered as a lived-through experience that unfolds in time (aesthetic) rather than as an exercise in extracting and taking away a range of facts or information from the text (efferent). Rosenblatt, too, is interested in the emotions stirred up in the reader by the text, and, as a believer in a Deweyan epistemology, seeks to bridge the gap between a knower and an object of knowledge, to heal the lesion caused by the New Critical tendency to view the text as the ultimate determiner of meaning.

These simplified summaries of the Fish, Holland, and Rosenblatt positions raise the possibility that writing one's autobiography or writing autobiographically engages a conception of knowledge as a function of reflective self-consciousness and of the active construction and reconstruction of personal experience. When cast in these terms autobiography can be conceptualized as a narrative undertaking focused on the events of an individual's life that supports a view of the knowledge so gained as at once personal, active, and experiential.

It is this latter idea that should be kept in front of us as we begin to explore the different sites of inquiry in education that have relied on and continue to rely on autobiography to guide and inform their enterprises. In the meantime, however, we will move away from Hirst's rational approach and toward Dewey's pragmatic and instrumental view of knowledge in order to subject the claims made thus far to further scrutiny. As well, we will inquire into whether the autobiographical urge to self-understanding and self-construction can be sustained in the manner here suggested.

Dewey and the Social Construction of Knowledge

The figure of John Dewey will loom large in these pages because aspects of his theories can still be found hovering over many areas of education. Consistent with his own intellectual move away from Hegel and toward Darwin, Dewey's theory can be said to have evolved over the entire course of his long life; it is therefore difficult to do more than indicate in a general way some aspects that seem to account for his beliefs.

Fittingly for our interest in autobiography, Dewey wrote an autobiographical essay entitled "From Absolutism to Experimentalism" (1960a) on the occasion of his 70th birthday, in which he retrospectively constructed his early intellectual movement from Hegelianism to his espousal of the naturalism of Darwin's theory. For Dewey, the fascination with Hegel lay in Hegel's notion of "an 'organic relation' in which the 'empirical consciousness' of the particular man and the objects of knowledge are embraced by a larger living whole, the 'universal consciousness'" (Zendler, 1960, p. 60). According to Morton White (1943), the Hegelian basis for Dewey's rejection of dualistic perspectives that separate a knowing subject from the object of knowledge allowed Dewey to convert, under Darwin's influence,

> . . . the universal consciousness into nature, the individual into the organism, and the object of knowledge into environment. The result, translated into naturalistic terms, is that the organism and its environment are both parts of nature. It follows that whatever

holds true of nature in general, holds true of human organisms in particular, and that the activity or capacity known as "knowledge," appears in man in accordance with the principles of organic evolution. (p. 46)

For Dewey, the revolutionary aspects of Darwin's thinking meant the denial of the fixed, the absolutely permanent. In this way he went against the Cartesian position of basing knowledge on certain beliefs or on intuitive knowledge. As Quinton (1977) expresses it, "the task of epistemology [was] not to give an account of secure and certified knowledge but rather of rational and warranted belief" (p. 3). In addition, this effort to come to grips with both the affective and cognitive factors of human consciousness resulted in a theory of interest in which the cognitive aspects of consciousness inform us and the emotional aspects "express the value or interest that this information has for the self, that is, it implies that an idea is not just a colorless fact but is also a way in which the self is affected" (Quinton, 1977, pp. 15–16). As a result, the knower, this seeker after warranted belief, is an active being, "an experimenter, not . . . a contemplative theorist" (Quinton, 1977, p. 3).

One final feature of Dewey's epistemology must be considered, namely, the idea that the pursuit of warranted belief is essentially a social process, and not, as might appear from this exposition, a solitary project. For it to be so would be to cast the knower in the isolated and solipsistic position implied by Descartes' continually doubting the contents of his own mind. On the contrary, knowledge is always a social product made up of what Dewey called funded experience, so that each individual need not start from the epistemological equivalent of reinventing the wheel.

Dewey claims that only when students are able to recognize themselves as in some way connected to the object of attention can they in any sense be said to know it. For many students, perhaps all, a primary object of attention and interest is the self; and to construct the self means to pursue the consequences of inquiry or active experimentation into or on that self, to discover how it has evolved and how it is situated or might be situated in society. The autobiographical impulse to write the self, as well as providing access to the forms of knowledge, supplies the warrant for providing and pursuing those autobiographical activities mentioned before that were designed to engage the student in the process of constructing and reconstructing the self in language.

Dewey's theories and ideas will receive more extensive treatment in a subsequent chapter. What has been undertaken here in a preliminary way is an attempt to show that the common-sense approach to autobiography as writing the self involves dealing immediately with issues that are fundamental to educational and curricular discourse as a whole, whether one views autobiography as an element in a text, as a method, or as a product. Hirst and Dewey demonstrate that autobiography as a process taken up by students in order to read and write about their lives and experiences embodies distinct forms of categorial knowledge into which students are to be immersed. But more importantly, perhaps, the student's self might be considered an object of inquiry or experiment, hence turning the writing of autobiography and autobiographical discourses into a way of thinking, a conceptual instrument of cognition. In this sense the view of knowledge implied in the effort to write the self is pragmatic in character, in that knowledge, like the self, comes to be seen as provisional, changing, and socially constructed.

In the rest of the chapter I will examine three examples of autobiography in education that exemplify not only its range and scope, but that support the contention that it exists in an undertheorized state generally, and in particular by some of those who wish to lay claim to its special properties. In order of inspection these sites are: language arts, in particular the work of James Britton; teacher education and research into teaching; and, finally, curriculum studies as theorized by the so-called "reconceptualists."

James Britton and Language Education

Fittingly enough for one who has been concerned with ideas of the way in which humans represent the world to themselves, how they construct their world representations and maps of experience, Britton, in his masterwork *Language and Learning* (1970a), begins with a personal reminiscence, an autobiographical fragment from which he moves on to provide a boldly eclectic theory of language and experience. By drawing on the work of Cassirer (1944), Harding (1937, 1962), Kelly (1963), and Langer (1960), Britton theorizes the ways in which talk and writing function for pupils to bring about a personal context for whatever the pupil is to learn. This kind of talk Britton calls *expressive speech*, speech that is close to the self of the speaker. It is also inherently social in character and sustains the notion that learning from each other and learning with each other are inextricably woven together. This view undercuts the idea that learning is the mere acquisition of inert knowledge; rather, it involves in Britton's

(1970b) words "a process of making finer and finer distinctions, and so building a more and more complex picture of the world" (p. 12).

From Kelly's (1963) theory of personal constructs Britton extracted the idea (traceable back through Kelly to the pragmatic instrumentalism of Dewey) of "man-the-scientist" [sic] (p. 4), wherein human behavior can be considered as an ongoing experiment: Like the scientist we draw from past experiences certain hypotheses that pertain to any present encounter and go about testing them and reforming them in the light of what actually happens. Britton uses Kelly's theory to further warrant his conception of the roles of participant and spectator, roles for which Britton had earlier found support in the work of Harding (1937, 1962). In those essays, Harding advanced the idea that man uses language for two distinct purposes: to have an effect on his actual world and to test ideas about that world without having to commit himself through action. In this way language in the role of the spectator is related to expressive speech, or gossip about events.

Britton has commented extensively on the relationship between the roles, functions, and categories mentioned above and their consequences for the development of learning and of writing abilities in particular. Even though Britton has ventured few specific comments on the subject of autobiography itself, the few he has offered make it clear that for him autobiography stands in direct relation to the very process of learning itself. For example, by telling our life stories "we shape our lives into a kind of narrative in order more fully to possess our experiences" (Britton, 1981, p. 7). In addition, it is precisely here that Dewey's influence makes itself felt. If in writing the self we "attempt to recapture, or at least to approximate to [sic], a natural order, an order found in living creatures" (p. 7), then through this action the student will not only discover a relatedness to society but will in fact discover the truth of the Herbartian doctrine that "ontogeny recapitulates phylogeny": the characteristics of the human race are to be found inscribed within each individual child. It is from a similar premise that Gunn (1982) deduces the conclusion that the autobiographical impulse is not really directed toward answering the question "Who am I?" but rather to the question *"Where do I belong?"* (p. 23, emphasis in original).

Britton's ideas are, of course, more complex than I have been able to indicate here; what this brief discussion shows is that Britton's project capitalizes on the child's autobiographical impulse to write the self, to construct a world representation of which the nucleus is the child's own experience.

Teacher Education, Teacher Thinking

The training of teachers and research into teaching can be considered together as activities that complement each other in numerous ways. On the one hand, teacher training courses are traditionally conceived of as avenues where the neophyte teacher is initiated into the rigors of lesson and unit planning as well as into the numerous practical techniques that will ensure survival in the real world of classrooms. On the other hand, research into teaching takes the classroom and the individually situated and experienced teacher as the starting point. It wants to conceptualize the nature of a teacher's personal practical knowledge, "that knowledge which can be discovered in both the actions of the person, and, under some circumstances, by discourse or conversation" (Clandinin, 1985, p. 362). In each case both practitioners and researchers rely on the insights afforded by the writing of autobiography. As a method it works in the first instance to reclaim hidden or forgotten aspects of an individual's past in order to prepare that individual for the classroom, and in the second instance to clarify practicing teachers' understanding of the amalgam of experience and knowledge that goes into the way in which they operate in the classroom.

For a practitioner like Abbs (1976), teacher preparation courses that begin by asking students to reflect on their own educational background harbor "the seeds of a great design" (p. 143). However, the seeds have been prevented from germinating owing to the constraints imposed by the timetable and by other institutional practices that militate against its use. Abbs wants to advocate framing the teacher preparation year around a course in autobiography in the face of critics who would argue for disseminating to the students more empirical knowledge from the social sciences and for introducing them to the practical problems of the classroom. Abbs (1976) bases his own argument on the proposition that *"True knowledge is existential knowledge"* (p. 149, emphasis in original); that is, if education is defined as "that power within experience which seeks to develop, refine, increase and deepen those truths created by experience" (p. 147), then the autobiographical act stands poised to reveal to the student the web of connections that "draws self and world together in one evolving *gestalt*" (p. 148). Thus the temporal dimension of autobiography, concerned as it is initially with past experience, is written from the perspective of the present and stands poised to assist the writer in making hypotheses or predictions about the future. By setting the student the task of "ploughing the field of his own experience" (Abbs, 1976, p. 148), Abbs considers that the student will then come to believe the truth of the proposition that all knowledge is existential knowledge and can never simply, *pace* E. D. Hirsch (1987), be acquainted with an unconnected series of discrete bits of information. The student who is given the opportunity of writing autobiographically will, it is asserted, become a more responsive and responsible teacher, since this attempt to re-create the past will reveal "the intimate relationship between being and knowing, between existence and education, between self and culture" (Abbs, 1976, p. 148).

We will, of course, be returning to examine critically the work of Abbs and others who seek to justify teacher preparation courses on these kinds of premises. Yet what has been made clear is the claim that autobiography, as both the process of writing a narrative of experience and as the product of that process, is in many senses the royal road to the accumulation of insights that reveal the connectedness, the unity of an autonomous and transcendental self or ego. Research into teaching exemplified by the project of Butt and Raymond (1987, 1989) employs the narrative potential within autobiography as the basis for collaborative autobiography. Collaboration here does not signify joint authorship; rather, the production of counterbiographies provides a check against tendencies to exaggerate and also enables feelings of trust to build up within a community of interpreters and researchers. We can now begin to appreciate more clearly the force of our earlier contention that when various enterprises within education state that they are pursuing autobiography as a method, they are not all speaking of the same conception of autobiography. For Abbs, for example, it is *autos* or the self that is of primary interest, while Butt and Raymond, although cognizant of notions of selfhood, retain a correspondingly greater interest in the *graphein*, or possibilities for discovery within narration. What remains to be discussed is precisely the nature of the claims put forward by these enterprises and the extent to which our developing notions of autobiography can help us in evaluating these claims with more clarity and rigor.

Reconceptualization of Curriculum Studies

Our final site of inquiry is the movement within curriculum studies that has been called "reconceptualization." Historically speaking, the movement may be said to have gained momentum with the publishing of the volume *Curriculum Theorizing: The Reconceptualists* (Pinar, 1975), in which two major strands of current thinking on the curriculum began to emerge. On the one hand, theorists like Huebner (1975) and MacDonald (1975) began to argue for a mode of education which tried to steer a middle course between critics of neo-Marxist persuasion (Apple, 1979; Giroux, 1983, 1988) and critical theorists inspired largely by the work of Habermas (Schubert, 1986). On the other hand, there were those associated with traditions within humanism (Pinar, 1975; Pinar & Grumet, 1976) who drew on phenomenology and existentialism to emphasize the experiential and situated nature of all human action. In each instance both groups were united in criticizing conservative theorizing of the curriculum, exemplified by Tyler (1949) and his quest for behavioral objectives, as representing the worst aspects of a technological and bureaucratic approach to education. In Pinar's (1975) view reconceptualists sought to study "matters of temporality, transcendence, consciousness, and politics" (p. xiii). Consistent, then, with this attempt to place back on the curricular agenda all those dimensions of intuitive, personal, political, and social experience that they claimed were being neglected by empirical/analytical approaches, autobiography emerged as a methodological tool that allowed these curricularists to argue that only through heightened consciousness and individual self-understanding could a major goal of education be achieved.

The local specifics and aspirations of Pinar's autobiographical method, called *currere*, after the Latin root of curriculum as a course-to-be-run, will engage us more fully in a subsequent chapter. It is crucial here to bear in mind some of the more general aspects of reconceptualist thought, particularly the recurring themes of personal liberation, ideology critique, and spiritual and moral introspection, in order to be able later to situate the concern for autobiography within the nexus of activities that Greene (1975) has called "reflective self-consciousness" (p. 303). From this brief introduction to reconceptualist thinking we can begin to see how important the idea of the restitution of personal experience becomes if one is committed to challenging a view of the curriculum and curriculum construction that is driven by a positivistic, instrumental conception of education.

CONCLUSION

This introductory chapter has of necessity been synoptic in manner and execution. As a prologue it has sought to situate autobiography and the autobiographical impulse as a legitimate preoccupation within education and the curriculum, as well as to foreshadow specific moments and issues where further clarification is required to bring some coherence to the various claims made on its behalf. Clearly the concept is slippery and difficult to pin down with the kind of rigor and certainty that would satisfy the scientifically minded. And yet, as I have begun to argue, this sense of elusiveness is, paradoxically, a major source of its utility and strength. As we saw, whether we wish to justify its use at the level of program, or whether larger epistemological claims are being offered for it as an irreducible way of knowing, it contains within itself the capacity and potential to act as a heuristic device of fundamental importance for a wide variety of educational projects. Although not itself a principle or a theory, autobiography permits access to valid sources of information that facilitate the recovery and inspection of ideas of great relevance to education and to the field of curriculum in particular. And yet, if autobiography exists in the minds of educators at large in an undertheorized state, we might wish to inquire if it is more adequately theorized in another field of inquiry, one from which we might be able to gain a more secure grip on its special characteristics. As a literary genre, autobiography has been the focus of a highly sophisticated and voluminous body of theorizing; it would seem natural, then, to turn to literary theory in order to discern how autobiography has been perceived and wherein lies the source of its fascination.

The following chapter will range widely at a metatheoretical level over some major critical statements that have sought to outline the specific nature of the genre. While doing so, we ought to resist the temptation to transfer the insights gleaned from literary theory too slavishly over into education. However, I believe that under certain provisos and subject to argumentation, not only will a progressive appreciation for what has been said about autobiography clear away many of the misconceptions within education surrounding some of the claims made on its behalf, but it will also provide us with a source of further warrants for its use, as well as with the rudiments of a working vocabulary, one that will at least allow us to apply some critical leverage to the various sites of inquiry within education selected for inspection. As these sites are visited, then, our inspection will be guided by and grounded in the rich theoretical tradition made available to us within literary theory. And as a view-affording lens, autobiographical theory will bring sharply into focus areas in education and the curriculum that at present are often dimly perceived and understood.

2 Autobiography in Literary Theory

The attraction of autobiographies and journals, both the reading and the writing of them, may be precisely because they are not involved in the repudiation of tradition or in "deformation" as so much recent literature, but in apparent construction and conservation.
Martha Ronk Lifson, 1979

A greater understanding and appreciation for what has been said about autobiography would serve to clarify more precisely what is involved when a practitioner or theorist in education announces a reliance on autobiography as a process, a method, or a product. Simply stated, then, the question the present chapter is concerned to answer is, "What are the distinguishing features of autobiography that might assist educators in making a more accurate judgment of its use and potential?" For there is in a sense a double promise lurking in an answer to this question: that not only will a broader appreciation for the distinguishing marks of autobiography help to make more explicit which conception(s) of autobiography is at work in a given instance of educational practice, but also that a more comprehensive feel for autobiography will provide the conceptual basis for the kinds of critical questions educators might wish to put to whole projects or enterprises within education, questions intent on discovering the nature of the assumptions about autobiography that appear to be guiding those projects. In other words, educators simply need to know more about autobiography at a fundamental level and in a language that is at once accessible but that does not dilute or minimize the difficulties involved in making sense of such a contentious field of intellectual inquiry. It is, however, outside the immediate mandate for this chapter to employ our expanding notions of autobiography in ways that will pay immediate critical dividends; that will be the purpose of subsequent chapters. Rather, this chapter will "by indirections find directions out": The expositions and discussions entered into here will supply the terms and the conceptual lenses through which particular areas in the curriculum will be scrutinized as we visit each chosen educational site in turn.

THE STRUGGLE OVER A DEFINITION

Since autobiography has been the subject of voluminous theorizing, to which the 76-page bibliography in Spengemann's *The Forms of Autobiography: Episodes in the History of a Literary Genre* (1980) attests—and since approaches to autobiography have included literary criticism (Eakin, 1985; Egan, 1984; Fleishman, 1983), structuralism (Mehlman, 1974), phenomenology (Starobinski, 1980), speech-act theory (Bruss, 1976), "mythology" (Olney, 1972), psychoanalysis (Mazlisch, 1970), feminism (Benstock, 1988; Smith, 1987), and post-structuralism (Sturrock, 1977)—literary commentators themselves have been hard pressed to come up with a consistent set of principles that not only does justice to the richness of the genre, but that also provides a sense of its limitations and of its continually contested nature. In this respect, much critical ink has been spilled over what actually constitutes an autobiography and what will count as its defining characteristics. On this score, Carlock's essay did much to bring the question of an adequate definition for autobiography out into the open. In that paper, Carlock (1970) accused scholars themselves of helping to perpetuate the confusion, for it was scholars themselves "who, in undertaking to write about the so-called autobiography . . . helped to precipitate the uncertainty existing today concerning what actually constitutes an autobiography" (p. 340). Not that scholars had avoided trying to define autobiography; in fact, as Carlock notes, attempts at definition divided themselves, roughly speaking, into two opposing camps: the strict and loose constructionists. Strict constructionists, like Shumaker (1954), Bottrall (1958), and Pascal (1960), insisted that autobiography implied "a specific literary genre that [could] be defined in terms of purpose, materials, focus, form, scope, and length" (Carlock, 1970, p. 341), while loose constructionists, exemplified in the work of Greene (1968), contended that letters, journals, and diaries should be considered autobiography too, since "'it does not matter what form that record takes, they shade imperceptibly into one another'" (cited in Carlock, p. 341). The problem, as Carlock (1970) sees it, is that the literary scholar wants to "have his cake and eat it, too" (p. 342); he says, like Humpty Dumpty, "when I use a word it means just what I want it to mean—neither more nor less" (p. 342). Carlock's paper tries bravely but ultimately in vain to wrestle some sense of coherence out of positions that draw their lines of demarcation on strategic grounds. She falls back on the common-sense idea that in an autobiography an author is writing about the self; this definition, however, is immediately qualified and rejected when she reminds herself about the awkward notion of authorship, and this at a time when neither Barthes's (1977) nor Foucault's (1977) announcement of the "death of the author" had percolated into the consciousness of North American critics in the manner it was subsequently to do (see Chapter 7). For Carlock, searching the ruins created by this definitional wrecking crew, there remain three words: "The autobiography *is*" (p. 349). But is what? To that there is no answer, only another question. Will we, she asks, "sing a requiem for a noun slaughtered by Humpty Dumpty, or try to rescuscitate the dead word and outlaw the tribe of Humpty Dumpty?" (p. 349).

Carlock's frustration at failing to discover a definition of autobiography that was neither determined by a particular critic's immediate purpose nor reduced to meaninglessness by a chain of qualifications, a string of "Yes, buts . . . ," is understandable and yet, in the last analysis, unnecessary. Understandable, because, seeking the kind of certainty many people turn to definitions to provide, critic and common reader alike can then go in search of the genuine article, the real autobiographical McCoy. But this kind of search is in the long run counterproductive, for it assumes that a definition alone can provide the kind of prima facie warrant that will resolve anomalies by reducing them to the adjudicating power of a definition. More productive, perhaps, than speculating on what an autobiography is, might be to embrace uncertainty and turn instead to orienting oneself in the possibly vertiginous task of mapping the struggle over the term, of attempting to come to grips with the manifold ways in which some individuals have given instrumental credence to the concept. In this way we will be required neither to sing a requiem nor to expel beyond the pale, but rather to join in an ongoing conversation that will give due attention to the shifting and contested character of the concept itself. By approaching the task from this perspective, the discoveries made in the genre will proceed more modestly if more dangerously by attempting to keep many conflicting ideas about autobiography in play, at the same time as we resist the temptation to settle for long on a list of unchanging givens. Therefore, in what follows, some effort will be made to steer the difficult course between the Scylla of the strict constructionist position with its reliance on definitions and confident assertions, and the Charybdis of the loose constructionist position for which autobiography is like a soft-sided suitcase, one capacious enough to accommodate all discourses that employ "the perpendicular 'I' " (Carlock, 1970, p. 341).

On account of these difficulties, then, this chapter will be given over to sifting through the statements of some representative figures who have likewise attempted to forego the appeal of definitions, and who have turned toward other principles of selection in order to provide themselves with an organizational framework within which they might be able for a moment to capture some of autobiography's protean characteristics. What will emerge, then, are a number of major statements regarding the nature of autobiography, statements educators can use either as an introduction or as a supplement to their own understanding and knowledge of the form.

From Life to Mind to Text

A logical place to begin might be with Spengemann's long bibliographic essay alluded to earlier. Spengemann (1980) undertook to write the essay for two important reasons: "to answer the need . . . for a review of the available scholarship and criticism" (p. 170), and "to dispel the notion . . . that nothing much has been written on the subject" (p. 170). And dispel the notion he does by providing annotated comments on articles and books written directly on the subject of autobiography, a list, incidentally, that excludes ancillary topics like theories of personality and identity, the place of autobiography in theories of narrative, theories of creativity, and psychoanalytic and biographical interpretations of literature. Spengemann begins by tracing the rise of autobiography as a scholarly topic. As such, he finds three distinct but "fundamentally related occurrences in the later nineteenth century: a sudden boom in the popular market for autobiographical writings of all sorts, an equally sharp rise in the number of essays on autobiography . . . and the publication of Wilhelm Dilthey's proposals for a study of human history based on the reading of autobiographical documents" (pp. 175–176). The common thread that runs through these three apparently unconnected occurrences is the idea that an individual life does add something to the evolving history of mankind and therefore individual lives are, potentially at least, of supreme interest to everyone, especially to the individual retelling the life story. In Spengemann's (1980) words, this is "the modern idea that human life does not reflect history, it *makes* it" (p. 176, emphasis in original).

The study of autobiography, unlike its production, progressed throughout the twentieth century in America and Europe, but largely in piecemeal fashion on both continents. Most of the work done in Europe was hardly known in North America and vice versa. And yet as that situation improved by the late 1960s with the publication of seminal works by Shumaker (1954), Pascal (1960), and others, the field became embroiled in problems of definition, of what to include and exclude from acceptance as "true" autobiography. For all that, however, several general but important trends were becoming apparent. Specifically, these were to be found in the change of emphasis within criticism from concentrating on the historical or biographical facts contained in the autobiography, "to the psychological states expressed in the text, [and] to the workings of the text itself" (Spengemann, 1980, p. 187). This displacement of critical interest from life to mind to text—"from facticity, to psychology, to textuality," as Spengemann (1980, p. 189) puts it—has not proceeded in steady nor uncontested fashion. The debate has in large measure oscillated between two poles. On the one side has been the debate over the position of autobiography relative to historiography, and on the other side, the position of autobiography relative to poetry (fiction). It is in effect the rediscovery at a different level of Goethe's *Dichtung und Warheit* (Truth and Poetry), truth here being construed as that found in the correspondence between the autobiographer's stated facts or information about his or her life (facts that should we so choose we can verify by empirical methods) and poetry or fiction, the idea that the very act of writing falsifies those facts by creating an order or pattern that never existed in reality. In addition, the view of autobiography as life history has led to its appropriation by scholars and researchers in the social sciences who, following Dilthey, considered it an instrument of knowledge and useful to their own disciplines, as well as a key source of information into the condition of groups in society like women, people of color, and immigrants, who, for one reason or another, have been forced to inhabit the margins of society (Morgan, 1978; Oakley, 1981). On the other hand, the notion of autobiography as primarily a literary form has led to heated debate into its governing conditions, conditions which, as we shall see, have been located both outside and inside the work in the cultural and personal situation of the autobiographer, and in the techniques, structure, and language of the work itself.

It is clear, therefore, that any inquiry into autobiography must take into account somewhere the tension between its historical and literary dimensions. To commit oneself to tracing the contours of these dimensions is to engage in separate tasks for the sake of clarity, while realizing that such an approach is simply an expository convenience and tends to blur the inextricable complementarity of both the historical and fictional elements. Here, Spengemann's essentially chronological approach in delineating the movement from life to mind to text is by no means the last word, nor the only principle of selection that might assist in organizing an inquiry into autobiography that might prove interesting to educators. Another approach may be found in Howarth's work (1980), in which he seeks to isolate elements or factors at work in all writing announcing itself as autobiography. In this instance, Howarth begins from the premise that the autobiographer's concerns are rhetorical and strategic; that is, the author (and in Howarth's case "author" very definitely includes painters from Raphael and Rembrandt to Hogarth and Van Gogh) begins with a decision "whether born of a master plan or born of frustration and anxiety" (Howarth, 1980, p. 86) that conditions the author's deployment of the medium (words, paint) and guides the selection of techniques that will give the work persuasive force and authority. As we shall see, Howarth, by borrowing and adapting Frye's (1957) elements of mythos, ethos, and dianoia (traceable of course back to Aristotle)—action, character, and theme—wants to hold fast to the idea that an author's autobiography is conditioned by his own and his audience's sense of what it means to work within certain literary or painterly conventions and assumptions.

Autobiography as Self-Portrait

Howarth (1980) proceeds from "a simple analogy: an *autobiography* is a *self-portrait*" (p. 85, emphasis in original). For Howarth, the self-portrait embodies many of the unique problems and ironies that can also be discovered within autobiography as a verbal artifact. By working with the connotations involved in the idea of composing, Howarth (1980) states that the artist's "costume and setting form the picture and also depict its form" (p. 85). Because the artist-model studies an image in a mirror, this places restrictions on what can be painted; for example, the artist cannot render the profile. Similarly, since when "he moves to paint a hand, the hand must also move" (p. 85), the artist is compelled to work from memory as well as from immediate vision, hence working on two levels of time and space. The end result is that the painterly process of self-portraiture is "alternately reductive and expansive; it imparts to a single picture the force of universal implications" (p. 85).

Now, although paint and words are dissimilar media that require different kinds of selection and arrangement, "vision and memory remain the essential controls, time and space the central problems, reduction and expansion the desired goals" (Howarth, 1980, p. 86). The verbal artist, however, by shaping a life into a self-portrait, arrives at a representation far different from the original model, since narrative as a technique employs a full range of rhetorical skills and devices in order to create the finished product. A reader, then, can study an autobiography as one would any other literary genre, by discovering and following the relationship between the verbal elements that go into its construction. Howarth's task is an attempt to isolate and identify those elements in a broadly generalizable way, and it is to a brief consideration of those elements that we now turn. As indicated, Howarth appropriates the Aristotelian categories of mythos, ethos, and dianoia, but modifies them to suit his purposes. Character and theme are offered as replacements for ethos and dianoia, while *technique* replaces mythos, the author's action, since "how he acts upon the narrative often overshadows how he acts *in* it" (1980, p. 86, emphasis in original).

The element of character is a tricky concept, since care must be taken to distinguish the character of the autobiography from the author himself. What is involved is a "double persona: telling the story as a narrator, enacting it as a protagonist" (p. 87). The key idea here is that although the artist and the model, the narrator and the protagonist, share the same name, they do not share "the same time and space" (p. 87). A moment's reflection convinces one of this. In an autobiography, we observe the life of the protagonist unfolding through time. In other words, the protagonist cannot know what the narrator knows, namely, his own future. For the sake of suspense and verisimilitude, then, the narrator must attempt to remain faithful to how he himself as protagonist is situated in time and space. However, the closer the narrative begins to approach the present, the closer the protagonist and narrator's thoughts and actions can begin to overlap.

The second element is the idea of technique, since it includes all of those devices of style, imagery, and trope that an author must have at hand if the verbal artifact is to be constructed from the inside out. For example, Howarth applauds the work of Starobinski (1980) on style in autobiography, since he has challenged the traditional notion that *le style c'est l'homme*, and has proposed instead that style is not subservient to content, not something added on, an adornment, but "a formal device significant in its own right" (Howarth, 1980, p. 87). To hold to this position is to believe that the simplest stylistic choices of tense or person are important, "since they lead to larger effects, like those of metaphor and tone" (p. 87). Finally, theme, "those ideas and beliefs that give an autobiography its meaning" (Howarth, 1980, p. 87), can emerge from a wide range of philosophical, cultural, or religious attitudes. The point to remember here is that since an author generally wrestles with large issues like the place in life of love, or disappointment, or loss, it could be held that, first of all, these themes are personal and involve the author alone. However, this would be to ignore completely the manner in which the author's own effort at coping with, say, disappointment or success might be representative of a general or universal tendency to approach those issues in a similar way. And second, this thematic element may help to account for the common fascination with autobiographies, might help explain a broad source of their appeal. Another source of that appeal may reside in seeing *the* theme of autobiography in its widest and most all-encompassing sense as nothing less than life itself. For if we subscribe to Shapiro's (1968) contention that "Autobiography is a comic genre in that it asserts the ego's transcendence of circumstances" (p. 449), then autobiography is essentially life-affirming in that it cannot legitimately end in death. One of the autobiographer's tasks, then, is to provide a sense of an ending that links the themes engaged by the life story with a more general perception of where those themes can touch the lives of the reading public.

For Howarth (1980), these three elements, although isolated to facilitate inspection, all work together to form "a single chain of relationships progressing from motive, to method, to meaning" (p. 88). By analyzing these elements we can become more aware of the writer's rhetorical strategies and hence, as critical readers, as opposed to readers who may not wish to travel that extra critical yard, we can begin to judge these particular achievements in comparison with other works, and so begin to expand our conceptions of the genre.

But although Howarth's framework is useful in providing a conveniently and conventionally manageable array of elements or axes, in the play of which we may discover both the author and ourselves, he does not suggest anything radically more provocative than that we remain aware that the protagonist is a fictional persona and by that awareness gain a clearer sense of the person behind the mask. Although it is equally apparent that Howarth has indeed supplied a highly plausible way to conceive of autobiography, his major purpose was to point out what makes autobiography a specifically *literary* genre. In other words, like many critics before him, he has attempted in one way or another to assimilate autobiography into the mainstream literary tradition, thereby hoping to stabilize it as a proper object of critical attention. Although it could be maintained that Howarth has attempted to deal with the rhetorical, personal, and thematic elements of the genre, I want to argue that he has not gone far enough in two other important directions.

He has not addressed adequately enough the elements within autobiography that single it out as a unique vehicle for the discovery and expression of historical consciousness, nor has he given any indication, as would feminist critics like Benstock or Smith, of the pervasiveness of autobiography as a mainstay of groups in a marginal relation to society as a way of reclaiming and celebrating alternative visions and aspirations for the individual in society. Howarth does hint at a wider audience for autobiography in his conception of theme, but in fact he does no more than uphold the traditional claim made for the humanizing effects of literature in general: that by representing the great themes of love, or death, or heroism, literature itself engages with and reveals unique truths about the human condition. This mimetic function again raises several related problems that concern not only the truth-value of autobiography, but the equally contentious areas of authorial purpose and intention, problems that will be taken up in more detail in the concluding chapter.

Therefore, in our search for principles that will allow us to select from the massive bulk of writing on autobiography those statements that somehow seem to address the needs of educators while remaining faithful to its status as a fluid mixture of history and fiction, we have tried on two approaches only to qualify them as less than fit for the purpose at hand. First of all, Carlock's approach to resolving the issue by means of calling for an all-embracing definition of what the phenomenon of autobiography is was rejected as ultimately chimerical, a vain attempt at gluing pieces of cracked eggshells together. Second, Howarth's approach, although it comes closer to providing the kind of broad principles that might be of interest to educators, seems to settle for espousing its purely literary qualities. It is evident, then, that as educators we would do well not only to take hold of a more thorough appreciation of autobiography as a literary genre, but that also, in our role as practitioners interested in the influences of society and culture on our endeavors, we have a responsibility to root out those largely neglected aspects of autobiography that speak directly to as wide a spectrum of subject disciplines and projects within the curriculum as possible.

Consequently, the remainder of this chapter will center its concerns around two major points of interest that will bring to our attention those statements within autobiographical theory that seem to address (with some inevitable overlap) these particular educational needs. These foci are, as foreshadowed earlier, the interplay between *history and fiction*, and between *high culture and minority culture*. In proposing these foci I am aware of the danger that any polarity is subject to being interpreted as offering only an either–or position, a position that I would argue is indeed both false and misleading. Rather, I want to stress that these positions are not binary opposites, but that since an educator's first interest is in looking for the special characteristics of autobiography that will prove of lasting value and utility in educational settings, and only second, perhaps, as an object of critical interest, then a way must be found to keep the dialectical movement implied by the word "interplay" alive and well. That will be the task of the following sections of this chapter.

THE CLAIMS OF HISTORY AND FICTION

In a carefully articulated appraisal aimed at balancing the competing claims of history and fiction within autobiography, Dodd's (1987) argument proceeds, like Carlock's, from the adversarial position that when different groups speak of autobiography this does not mean "that there is any common understanding of what autobiography signifies" (p. 61). For historians, autobiography is seen as a "sometimes unique source of experiences unrepresented in the dominant records of the past" (p. 51), while for literary critics autobiography is a "carefully sifted, sorted and graded selection . . . of literature, with its own pedigree stretching back to St. Augustine" (p. 61). Dodd expresses well the kinds of tensions that exist within literary theory, because one group, the historians, is intent on focusing on the relationship between the self and history, that is, in untangling the complex weave of a self and the events and circumstances that have gone into forming that self, while the other group, the literary critics, following a notion of autobiography-as-fiction, as a consciously crafted literary artifact, view the self as "the product of imagination rather than history" (Dodd, 1987, p. 64). Consequently, autobiography as an art "becomes a way of protecting the self from history" (p. 65). Thus any inquiry into autobiography, especially one whose objective is to provide educators and workers in curriculum with a more coherent sense of the field as well as with some of the concepts that are crucial to an understanding of the genre, must seek out statements on autobiography that clearly examine the boundaries of the genre and deal head-on with the interplay between history and fiction. We could do no better, then, than to take a close look at the work of Gusdorf (1980), Weintraub (1975, 1978), and Hart (1970). Gusdorf's seminal essay still stands as a landmark in contemporary thinking about the genre; Weintraub takes as his province the expression of historical consciousness implied in the form; while Hart provides a forceful and useful discussion of authorial intention, of the relationship between an author's purpose and his view of his audience. In other words, we will discover in these statements fundamental issues of truth, form, and intention that are unearthed in virtually any approach to autobiography from whatever ideological commitment. For ease of exposition and discussion, each writer's work will be considered in turn, with comments and observations interpolated as we proceed.

Gusdorf and the Limits of the Genre

Before considering Gusdorf's classic statement on autobiography, one caveat must be acknowledged. Susan Stanford Friedman (1988) believes that Gusdorf's work raises "serious theoretical problems" (p. 34) for all groups, especially women, who take a different view of self-creation and self-consciousness. Gusdorf's individualistic model is criticized by Friedman on two counts: first, that it does not deal with "the importance of a culturally imposed group identity for women and minorities" (p. 34), and second, that it "ignores the differences in socialization in the construction of male and female gender identity" (pp. 34–35). Thus, from both an ideological and psychological point of view Friedman claims that Gusdorf ignores the "*relational* identities" (p. 35, emphasis added) that are at work in the individuation processes of women and minorities. Although we cannot take up here the full import of Friedman's criticisms, we would do well to recall them to mind as a forceful corrective to much of the exposition that is to follow, as well as to indicate that her main points will be raised again in another context in the concluding chapter. For now, however, Georges Gusdorf's ground-breaking essay is the object of our attention.

Gusdorf (1980) begins by demonstrating how autobiography as a genre has not always existed, nor does it exist everywhere. As he states, "it would seem that autobiography is not to be found outside our cultural area; one would say that it expresses a concern particular to Western man" (p. 29). Autobiography exists when humanity begins to delight in its own image and thinks itself worthy of special interest. Gusdorf's use of metaphor is the clue here to his central point. On the one hand, his figurative language motions toward a moral economy of the self, wherein by narrating one's own life story one can save "this precious capital that ought not to disappear" (p. 29). On the other hand, the legalistic or, more provocatively, the evangelical metaphor advances the autobiographer as witness: "he calls himself as a witness for himself; others he calls as witness for what is irreplaceable in his presence" (p. 29).

This awareness of individuality is a late product of civilization, and Gusdorf theorizes that the isolated being was rarely the important unit. Gusdorf's myth is one of a lost organic community where each person was born into a social role; individuality, then, occurs when there is a fall from this role. Only under these conditions can identity and a wish to explore it become problematic. As he says, "Autobiography becomes possible only under certain metaphysical preconditions" (p. 30). Curiosity about the individual was a direct consequence of the Copernican revolution: our place in the cosmic cycle was replaced by the adventure of the autonomous individual. In this sense biography as a literary genre provides only the exterior of the person; if the person happens to be a "Great Man," his life is reviewed through the ideological lenses of the age and according to the demands of current propaganda. Autobiography implies a spiritual revolution: "The artist and model coincide, the historian tackles himself as object" (p. 31).

The notion here is that a subject who seizes on the self as object engages complex psychological mechanisms in which an individual encounters a double. However, this double is at once more fascinating and more frightening, since the individual perceives the self as both fragile and vulnerable. Narcissus is invoked in this instance as the archetypal figure, one who falls in love with his reflection mirrored in the pool. In this respect, Gusdorf does not fail to link the medieval perfection of silver-backed mirrors to a disruption in human experience; likewise, contemporary psychoanalysis of the Lacanian variety employs the idea of a mirror stage to account for the emergence within the infant's consciousness of his own personality. The ability to distinguish what is outside from what is within lies at the heart of the ability to shape one's own version of social reality. The person who believes that mirrors or photographs will somehow steal his soul is totally unlike the child who "has had all the leisure necessary to make himself at home with the changing garments of appearances that he has clothed himself in under the alluring influence of the mirror" (p. 33).

Although autobiography appeared in the Middle Ages and Renaissance in writing such as Augustine's *Confessions* and Montaigne's *Essais*, it is with the Romantic era that the rediscovery of autobiography may be said to have taken place. Ideas of individuality were then coupled with ideas of sincerity wherein telling all about the self became a positive virtue. Gusdorf begins to account for this by introducing the concepts of history and anthropology, concepts that will allow him to locate autobiography in its cultural moment. In order to accomplish this, Gusdorf must first make some crucial and critical distinctions between a historian of the self and an autobiographer.

The historian of the self is analogous to the painter who wishes to produce a self-portrait; however, as with the portraitist, the historian can only capture a moment of external appearance. The autobiographer, on the other hand, "reassemble[s] the scattered elements of his individual life and . . . regroup[s] them in a comprehensive sketch" (p. 35). As a painting is a representation of the present, an autobiography retraces a period, a development across time. Unlike the author of a private journal, who notes his impressions and mental states from day to day with only a minimal concern for continuity, the autobiographer is required to keep a distance with respect to himself "in order to reconstitute himself in the focus of his special unity and identity" (p. 35). If memoirs are always a "revenge on history" (p. 36), then the autobiographer's act of memory is carried out for its own sake, to "recover and redeem lost time in fixing it forever" (p. 37).

In this view of autobiography as intervention, the author assumes the task of reconstructing the unity of a life in time. Although Gusdorf knows that events both determine and place limits on any unity of attitude and action, there are "essential themes" (p. 37) of personality that impose themselves on the "complex material of exterior reality" (p. 37). Thus the anthropological prerogative of autobiography is clear: "It is one means to self-knowledge thanks to the fact that it recomposes and interprets a life in its totality" (p. 38). Autobiography as a "second reading of experience" (p. 38) is truer than the first reading because it adds consciousness of itself to the raw contingencies of experience. By invoking Hegel's dictum that "consciousness of self is the birthplace of truth," Gusdorf can then establish the fact that the passage from raw experience to consciousness in memory modifies the significance of the experience, a passage that not only can be sought again through time, but can be "rediscovered and drawn together again beyond time" (p. 39). Memoirs and confessions are not objective and disinterested, but are works of personal justification. Autobiography, which on the surface looks like an effort at retracing the history of a life, in fact hides a deeper intention. This is none other than "an apologetics or theodicy of the individual being" (p. 39).

But Gusdorf finds several basic problems with this ontological quest. The historian of the self, when coming to review the past, takes the unity and identity of the self for granted and imagines that he can "merge what he was with what he has become" (p. 39). However, a narrative consisting of memories composed after the event by someone who knows the outcome in advance cannot hope to capture this tension, this unfolding of the unknown. "Thus the original sin of autobiography is first one of logical coherence and rationalization" (p. 41). In this sense autobiography substitutes that which has been formed for that which is in the process of being formed.

For the autobiographer, this narrative problem is insurmountable: the narrator always starts knowing the outcome of the story in advance. It is because of the synoptic imperative within "true" autobiography that other forms such as daybooks and journals fail to convey the essence of a life, no matter how minutely ordered. These discourses are caricatures of real life; the attempt to capture life's flux is doomed to failure and becomes instead a sterile rendering of places, names, and dates. From this reasoning, Gusdorf adduces the principle that the significance of autobiography should be sought "beyond truth and falsity" (p. 43) as we might commonly conceive of these notions. Certainly, the historian has a right to check out an autobiographical narrative for accuracy; but a reader might with more profit view the narrative as a work of art and pay more attention to its stylistic harmony than to its faithfulness to the facts of the life itself. We therefore tolerate errors, omissions, even downright lies, in the service of discovering the truth of the individual. Yet as important as this lying in the service of truth purports to be, the literary function of autobiography is secondary when one compares it with the truth-claims of the anthropological approach. The motto here seems to be that in creating, one begins to be created: the liberating moments of self-creation are enacted in language, but language shaped according to a primary desire to elucidate the past, to draw out the structure of our being-in-time. The emancipatory, and one would have to say therapeutic, impulse behind this self-examination implies that we are no longer the people we were after our struggle to interrogate the essence of our being more intensely. So it is that we can with some justification alter the assertion that *le style c'est l'homme,* to *le style construit l'homme.*

In sum, then, Gusdorf concludes that it is not the task of autobiography to show us the stages of an individual's life—that should be left to the historian or biographer—but rather to reveal to us the effort of a creator "to give the meaning of his own mythic tale" (p. 48). There is never any end to individuals' dialogue with themselves in search of their own absolutes, the ground of their being. Instead, like Jacob, we continue to wrestle with our angels. In reality, however, we grapple only with ourselves, or with the shadow of a self that can never finally be taken hold of or subdued.

In spite of Gusdorf's ground-breaking work, many subsequent commentators seem to have suffered from collective amnesia when it comes to tracking down his essential point; namely, that the significance of autobiography was to be found in its anthropological rather than in its purely literary function as a genre. Gusdorf himself is, in part, responsible for this confusion, since he fell foul of his own mythic thinking in that he considered Narcissus the appropriate myth for the (literal) mirror-gazing autobiographer. The attractions of the Narcissus myth are easy to see; indeed, as Olney (1980) states, "This shift of attention from *bios* to *autos*—from the life to the self—was, I believe, largely responsible for opening things up and turning them in a philosophical, psychological, and literary direction" (p. 19). However, Gusdorf, although in part responsible for this shift of attention to the literary qualities of autobiography, never lost sight of its alternative, anthropological significance. What Gusdorf was really arguing for, and what educators in particular would seem to require, is a conception of autobiography that, in Gunn's (1982) words, is "sufficiently capacious to account for [it] as a human, cultural, and even a religious activity" (p. 10). Consequently (and this is a major point that will be reiterated throughout in different contexts), we might begin to consider an alternative myth to capture the essence of autobiography. To this end, Gunn (1982) suggests that Antaeus, rather than Narcissus, should guide our conception of the form. Under this conception, the self that comes to life is not that of Narcissus, who drowned reaching for his mirror-image in the pool, but rather Antaeus, who, so long as he remained in touch with the earth, could not be killed. Hercules, learning his secret, suspended Antaeus in the air and hence was able to overcome him. As Gunn (1982) puts it, "Understood as the story of Antaeus, the real question of the autobiographical self then becomes *where do I belong?* not, who am I? The question of the self's identity becomes the question of the self's location in a world"

(p. 23, emphasis in original). To assist in perhaps redressing the balance away from the specific literary claims for autobiography by following through on this notion of worldliness, of grounding the self in its historical and cultural contexts, we can move now to the work of Karl Weintraub.

Weintraub and Historical Consciousness

As befits the reflections of a self-styled "simpleminded historian" (Weintraub, 1975, p. 821), Weintraub is anxious to situate more precisely the emergence of autobiography as a major Western preoccupation. He locates the use of the term in Germany shortly after 1800, and notes that its first usage in English, according to the *Oxford English Dictionary,* was in an 1809 article in the *Quarterly Review* by Robert Southey. Thus autobiography and its cultural function are seen as part of the "intellectual revolution" (p. 821), which also saw the emergence of the "modern form of historical mindedness we call historism or historicism" (p. 821). For Weintraub, the essence of autobiography is "concretely *experienced* reality and not the realm of brute external fact" (p. 822, emphasis in original). Biography, on the one hand, reverses the process of deriving value from the inward absorption of external fact by trying to discern the inner structure of a life from data on outward behavior or conduct, or from statements about that inner life. In other forms such as memoirs or reminiscences, the writer's eye is focused less on the inner experience and more on the recording of external facts and events. On the other hand, autobiography, if it is to be more than an account of what Weintraub calls the "I-and-its-circumstances" (p. 824), must adhere more closely to its real subject matter—character, personality, self-conception—"all those difficult-to-define matters which ultimately determine the inner coherence and meaning of a life" (p. 824). "Real" autobiography, then, must be an interweaving of self-consciousness and experience, and all centered upon "an aware self aware of its relation to its experience" (p. 824).

Weintraub is certain that the genuine autobiographical impulse stems primarily from a point of view, "a co-ordinate point in space and time at which the autobiographer stands to view his life" (p. 824). Second, this point of view is located somewhere beyond a moment of crisis or a set of experiences that approximate the same function as a crisis. From Augustine to Rousseau, Vico to Goethe, all experienced some point of crisis at which time their lives underwent a wrenching. At this nodal moment the course of a life is seen to have connecting lines that were previously hidden; a new direction becomes clear where only wandering existed before. Weintraub stresses that during this crisis the writer's retrospective view discerns a *pattern* in experience; otherwise the autobiographical function becomes mere self-orientation, a function that would result in the form being "crippled or undeveloped" (p. 825). Where self-discovery or self-orientation predominates, the genuine autobiographical act of seeing the essential wholeness of a life is missing. Once this point of view has been gained, the writer "imposes on the past the order of the present" (p. 826). This results in facts being "placed into relationships retroactively in which they did not stand when they were first experienced" (p. 826). These facts are singled out because they are seen to have some symptomatic meaning they did not possess before. Past life is therefore being rearranged, or as Weintraub would have it, retrospectively interpreted, in terms of the meaning that life is now seen to hold. "The dominant autobiographical truth, therefore, is the vision or pattern or meaning of life which the autobiographer has at the moment of writing his autobiography" (p. 827).

But if this view stresses the temporal dimension inherent in the autobiographical act, it also conceals the notion that the writer is likely to have been conditioned by prevailing ideas of what the word "life" means. If one of the hallmarks of life is that it is a process, then autobiography may have a special function in helping us to understand its dynamics. In this task there is a need, as Weintraub states, "to balance diachronic and synchronic elements" (p. 829), since both are required to comprehend how an individual developed through time. Here, self-portraiture must be subsumed under the prior imperative of viewing life-as-process. To have introduced the idea of a life that develops or unfolds is to place in the foreground the tendency within autobiography of recapturing that process in narrative. If one emphasizes the ideas of a Human nature, then the notion of unfolding comes into play. What is present from the beginning, in embryo as it were, gradually unfolds as if by predetermined necessity. For example, once the moment of crisis has been experienced, as with Augustine, life can be seen as the unfolding of the Creator's design for him that he was previously too blind to see. On the other hand, in the figure of Rousseau, we observe the concept of life as a development through time. For Rousseau, civilization corrupted the unfolding of the naturally good, and so he explored the conditions that would have to prevail if individuals were to translate their potential into actual life. In the words of Weintraub's memorable sentence, "In living with one's world, one forms a self as the world moves on, and one helps form a world as oneself is being formed" (p. 833). Thus, if auto-biography is a historical genre that retrospectively interprets a signif-icant portion of a life, it behooves us to attend to the underlying as-sumptions of a writer regarding the process of a life as it interacts with the world. In this way we will begin to view autobiography as a genre that contains powerful historical and social dimensions.

Another of Weintraub's major contentions is that "The manner in which men conceive of the nature of the self largely determines the form and process of the autobiographic writing" (p. 834). If a person is seen as a creature with a fixed potential, then the history of autobi-ography is the story of an effort to attain the true form of Humanity. "One form of self results in one form of autobiography" (p. 834). But if we posit Humanity's protean nature, then the history of the genre becomes the story of Humanity's changing conception of the self. Likewise, the history of self-conceptions can also assist in the explo-ration of different cultural configurations. If this is so, then autobiog-raphy not only aids our understanding of history, but again helps us to understand life as continuous process.

One other item of significance for autobiography is the tend-ency within cultures to compress their essential values and con-ventions into models of human behavior. Thus, in the process of self-formation, individuals constantly have before them concrete ex-amples or models of being. However, in every instance these words exert greater power because of their wider, more universal applica-tion. When individuals wish to dedicate their lives to the attainment of an ideal, they can find immediate guidelines in a model. In this way, the story of a person's life can be fitted into some basic archetypal form, for example, the stoic, the cynic, the saint. Weintraub states that "models are of particular importance in youth and adolescence" (p. 838), yet the dominant personality conception of Western man does not fit the model type, but is in fact antithetical to it.

Since the Renaissance, the ideal has been captured in our notion of the individual. Under this conception, the individual is all; one must be true to one's own "self." Decisions about life must be based on their appropriateness to that conception of oneself. When a person is possessed by a consciousness of individuality, there is no room for role-playing, nor does that person want to compress an autobiogra-phy into a "prepressed formal literary frame" (p. 839). It is in this discussion of the emergence of the individual in history that Wein-traub signals the overriding thesis of his paper: "The development of autobiography as a necessary cultural form for giving expression to personal history went hand in hand with this turn towards individuality" (p. 841).

Yet this individual self-searching is made more complex today as different cultures (and subcultures) present different models, and as the world splinters and diversifies into national and personal lifestyles. One method of coping with this overload is to regain a sense of history, to review the autobiographies of men and women who wrote from more traditional conceptions of personality. To do so is to uncover in more pristine form the "variegated richness of consciousness" (p. 843), and to prepare the ground from which a deeper and truer understanding of individuality can flourish.

Weintraub concludes his paper with a plea not only for a fuller appreciation of the historical dimension in the relationship between autobiography, consciousness, and individuality, but for the sociological and moral aspects of it as well. By becoming a literary form in which individuality could best account for itself, autobiography obtained a cultural function it did not possess before. This self-conscious cultivation was the same thing "as living in the world with historical consciousness of the world" (p. 847). But since we are above all social beings, bound to society and culture in innumerable ways, "real" self-cultivation involves a concomitant responsibility to the world. Such a sense of social responsibility will cure us from all narcissistic leaning, and return our gaze toward finding how, through our self-examination, society may be improved.

It is worth remarking here in passing, from the point of view of educators and educational theorists, that whereas Weintraub ultimately moves beyond the notion of models as a guide for living or as archetypes after whom one might shape one's own autobiography, the educational value of models must not be dismissed so quickly. For example, Egan (1988) builds his argument for a bold new conception of early childhood education around the idea of mythic understanding, a sense-making capacity that he considers one of the *bonnes à penser* (literally, "good things to think with"), which are neither mental characteristics nor forms of knowledge, but "capacities that are evoked, stimulated, and developed in becoming initiated into the forms of sense-making available in a particular culture" (Egan, 1988, p. 170). An engagement with autobiography, whether at the level of reading or writing, is not only an initiation into specific forms of consciousness and experience, but also discloses one of autobiography's key functions: the exploration of the struggle of individuals to adapt to the environment or to work on that environment to transform it to fit their own needs. In support of this, we might consider the cogency of one of Shapiro's (1968) major points: If there is a close relationship between "the psychological patterns that integrate a life and the symbolic . . . themes that integrate autobiography" (p. 447), then not only does autobiography testify to the power of models, but more importantly, "it participates in the cycle of incarnations by becoming a model itself" (p. 448). Autobiography, as a story of recognizing one's place in the world and of one's struggle to adapt to it or to change it, may require at a particular stage of development the (emblematic) testimony of individuals who themselves were engaged in a similar struggle. And as Shapiro (1968) states:

> We must have models, roles, myths, attitudes to identify with, because they enable us to structure time, to shield ourselves from inner and external chaos, prepare the next move. By identifying with models, consciously and unconsciously selecting and rejecting, we synthesize the self that best conforms to our ruling pattern, without ceasing to be recognizable and typical. (p. 448)

We will, of course, have more to say later about the importance for education of recognizing this dimension within autobiography; for now, however, we must turn to the work of Francis Hart in order to shore up our understanding of the idea of intentionality, of an author's purpose for writing an autobiography.

Hart and Evolving Intentions

For Hart (1970), "every autobiography can appropriately and usefully be viewed as in some degree a drama of intention" (p. 492): a drama because, as writers, the constant problem is one of selecting a role which, as protagonist, the writers can inhabit in order to project or display their own particular version of themselves. And as readers or interpreters, we must remain aware of the constantly shifting pattern of scenes and situations, alive to the symbolic or thematic possibilities occasioned by a narrator's selective memory. Hart (1970) maintains that the formal principles in autobiography "evolve and fluctuate as autobiographical intentions interact and shift" (p. 491) to the extent that he believes these fluctuating intentions can best be understood when one can isolate as a *predominant* concern whether the autobiography is essentially a confession, an apology, or a memoir. In order to clarify what follows, I would like to quote Hart (1970) at length as he defines for us the post-Enlightenment connotations of these terms.

"Confession" is personal history that seeks to communicate or express the essential nature, the truth of the self. "Apology" is personal history that seeks to demonstrate or realize the integrity of the self. "Memoir" is personal history that seeks to articulate or repossess the historicity of the self. . . . Confession is ontological; apology, ethical; memoir historical or cultural. (p. 491)

Now, of course, none of these categories is either strict or neatly self-contained, but in fact may be more usefully viewed as they interact, conflict, or complement each other. Together, however, they seem to be able to account for the *autos*, or self (confession), as well as the *bios*, the life, the past (apology, memoir).

The important point here to remember is that these complementary categories are component parts of the autobiographical process whether life is viewed, like J. S. Mill's, from the relative calm after a period of crisis, or whether the writer remains silent, like Freud, about any event in his life that had no bearing on the progress of psychoanalysis. In each case it matters how a writer begins to work out his own "fluctuating mixture of confession, apology, and memoir" (Hart, 1970, p. 488). In other words, we must resist the temptation to light on confessions, apologies, or memoirs as different kinds of autobiography; rather, they are different kinds of autobiographical intentions. The categories are useful to the extent that they enable readers and writers to witness how, depending upon the events that have been selected, and depending upon the role(s) the author thinks it fit to adopt, this drama of intentions evolves. Nor is this all. To bear in mind the shifting terms of this drama is to further resist the temptation to see the life displayed in static terms, as a body-at-rest after a lifetime of struggle. This would be to settle for a stricter definition of autobiography than has been suggested throughout this chapter, to settle on seeing a life whole as *the* characteristic of "true" autobiography. To the contrary, when we posit the notion of a writer's fluctuating intentions, we thereby lend credence to the possibility that a particular fragment of a life, written with whatever autobiographical intention, incurs the figurative force of metonymy in its relationship to that life: that the characteristics of the whole may be discovered in the specifics of the part.

Hart's work, therefore, serves to loosen up the tight rein that searching for an author's final intention has over literary interpretation generally, and particularly over autobiography where the author-as-protagonist is supposed to know from the inside out what has gone into giving that life its special shape and characteristics. We are enjoined to consider that shape or pattern as something that evolves or is discovered *in* the act of writing, something that operates through the interplay of history and fiction and is revealed as each autobiographer "wrestles with options of truth and integrity in the recovery of his personal history" (Hart, 1970, p. 511).

HIGH CULTURE/MINORITY CULTURE

The point has been reached in our discussion where we must break off our encounters with commentators whose primary aim was to argue, if not for a strict constructionist conception of autobiography, then for taking autobiography seriously as a legitimate literary form. To this end, there is little doubt that these critical exercises have fulfilled that singular purpose, to the extent that, as Dodd (1987) argues, they have indeed identified, but may not finally have stabilized, the place of autobiography within the Tradition. One continuing sign and measure of that instability resides, as we saw, in the dialectical interplay between autobiography-as-history and autobiography-as-fiction. It was argued that what might constitute a critical loose end for literary theorists was of great strategic and instrumental importance for those in education, since education requires a more capacious notion of autobiography, one that is faithful to its general characteristics and intentions, while at the same time allowing for the possibility of deploying it with consistency and coherence within an expanding number of educational contexts. This looser conception is captured in the phrase "high culture/minority culture " and was introduced in order to signify that what Gunn (1982) and others call "the autobiographical impulse" (p. 12) should not be considered solely the province of self-styled artists, but could be discovered at work among, for instance, oppositional and marginalized groups as a way of representing and reclaiming their own experience and sense of solidarity (see Benstock, 1988; Smith, 1987). What must now be considered more fully is Rockwell Gray's (1982) argument that we are currently living in an age when self-exploration is all but mandatory, and that signs of an autobiographical impulse can be found woven into the very fabric of society. In other words, if we are to believe social critics and historians like Rieff (1959) and Lasch (1978), that we are living in a "therapeutic" or "narcissistic" culture, then autobiography is one way of contributing toward "a general sense of release which accompanies the full-fledged legitimation of self-display" (Gray, 1982, p. 39). Gray's (1982) discussion of the state of autobiography now, which as we shall see makes interesting and provocative mileage out of a loose constructionist position, proceeds from the following proposition: "That autobiography is not the undertaking of a select few, but a general form of thought, a specific twist of culture which is manifest every time anyone turns to the autobiographical mode of conduct" (p. 42).

Gray (1982) strikes the keynote for his argument by seeking to locate contemporary expressions of the autobiographical impulse in the "myriad corners" (p. 31) of society beyond the "clearly demarcated format of books" (p. 31). Although locations can still be discovered in books, especially on the racks in drugstores, where every so-called public figure in entertainment, sports, or politics is cashing in on autobiography as a spectator sport, the autobiographical impulse also conditions our speech and the ways in which we make sense of the world. But Gray (1982) detects in this search for personal voice, this quest for identity, a tacit and more sinister dimension. This rage for autobiography is also an "admission of powerlessness, for one turns everything into personal history only when one fears that some larger collective history has no place for one" (p. 32). However, as a way of situating oneself existentially, autobiography continues to privilege and give voice to the "still, sad music of humanity" amid the racket and cacophony of the hucksters for whom unburdening themselves in public is undertaken to the accompaniment of cash register bells.

For Gray (1982), then, regardless of the kinds of judgments one might wish to make about the motivations behind much autobiographical writing, it is sufficient to understand that in this looser conception, autobiography refers "to any reflective effort made in the interest of restoring meaning, purpose, and value to one's life" (p. 33). Nor does this reflective effort necessarily need to assume the shape of a conscious literary product; dance, film, painting, even music can be considered equally valid vehicles for the process of reflection. Furthermore, we must rid ourselves of thinking that autobiography is engaged in at an advanced age in summative fashion; autobiography can be undertaken "at almost any age and, potentially, as many times as one chooses" (p. 34).

If autobiography is to be reconceived of in this looser sense as a way of coping with or understanding one's life that can be done at any time and in any number of forms, then it might be objected, as we saw in Chapter 1, that this borders on a kind of discursive anarchy, and that the term then becomes so diffuse as to virtually disappear. But as was argued earlier and requires repeating here, there are compelling epistemological reasons for embracing the paradoxical notion that autobiography's greatest strength is to be found in precisely that sense of diffuseness and attenuation. As autobiography spills over to color the conditions of our everyday lives, it will often be employed in ways that are more meretricious than meritorious. In this instance, Gray (1982) argues for actively seeking out the specific "conditions and setting which promote or curtail acting, writing, speaking, or even thinking autobiographically" (p. 36). Under this scenario, for example, one can place oneself in situations that are designed to call forth meditations on one's life. They might stretch from poring over family photographs in fifth grade to constructing narratives of our educational experiences in graduate courses. In each case these situations promote or generate autobiographical reflection; they are, in Gray's (1982) inelegant but useful phrase, "autobiorevelatory choices" (p. 36). By means of these, that metonymic part–whole relationship between a moment in one's life and the larger vision of one's life as a whole might become a series of "personal time capsules" (p. 36) from which will emerge important aspects of one's experience that can provide the forms for self-reflection. Autobiography as a form of thinking does not necessarily imply the design and construction of the big picture of one's life, but through the use of episodic memory the dramatization of selected vignettes from the past may be sufficient to occasion that penetration into the slippery notion of reality that is our own experience.

Taken under the terms of Gray's argument, then, the autobiographical impulse can be seen to attach itself to a diverse number of forms, all given over to the aim of self-understanding. Autobiography, as a cultural mode, does answer a complex range of human needs. It is "an order we give to culture and a shape which, reciprocally, culture gives to us" (Gray, 1982, p. 43). Regardless of whether we concur with the idea that the autobiographical impulse has grown in direct proportion to our collective feelings of helplessness, anomie, and loss of group solidarity, autobiography is a way in which one might begin to articulate, to revision, however tentatively, the contours that make up the map of our world representation. In this sense it retains much of its original sixteenth- and seventeenth-century spiritual flavor of Protestant soul-searching; only rather than monitoring the pilgrim's progress toward heaven, or indeed subscribing to the belief in an essential self or soul, secular autobiography journeys into the heart of darkness in the belief that this journey will enable the individual to gain some ultimate sense of meaning from the world.

Redemption here, undertaken in the service of that autobiographical impulse, is motivated by the belief that the deeper one penetrates into the unique characteristics of one's own situation, "the closer [one will] come to transpersonal meaning, to connecting with others, with posterity, with humanity as a whole" (Gray, 1982, p. 46). To do so is to become progressively aware of the distinctions among (to borrow from Jung) memories, dreams, and reflections, which serve the utilitarian end of orienting us to the dictates and contingencies of the world. In addition, to participate in that collective unconscious should remind us constantly, like Antaeus, of our grounding in the world and in its struggles and responsibilities.

Finally, if we in education are encouraged under this looser conception of autobiography to assume the role of archaeologist and begin to construct ourselves and our future projects from fragments and shards of memory and time, then we can begin to see how the prevailing psychological models of human nature can ultimately be reconciled with a broader spectrum of socially identifiable goals. These goals need not involve the individual in a process of adaptation in any pejorative sense; rather, over the shoulder of the sometimes alien face that stares back from the mirror, we need to become aware that a cultivated landscape or social group is always a part of the topographical features framed by our self-portraits.

CONCLUSION

This chapter began by posing a question regarding the benefits that educational theory and practice could expect to gain from a more thorough understanding of autobiography. From that discussion some answers emerged that drew attention to two major points of emphasis within virtually any theory of autobiography: the dynamic interplay between history and fiction, and that between high culture and minority culture. These groupings followed to some degree Carlock's distinction of statements that fall into either a strict or loose constructionist view of autobiography. Throughout, it was argued that, although the temptation persists to consider autobiography as a purely literary genre and hence to concentrate on its characteristics as literature, the existence of autobiography as a popular form that also partakes in myriad ways of the autobiographical impulse militated against any such narrow conception. In other words, neither the literary/high cultural form nor the historical/minority cultural form can exist for long in complete isolation. Since the autobiographical urge spills over to inform any number of ways of making sense of life and experience, it was argued that the long-term benefits for educational theory and practice must be sought in the context of the continuing interplay and cross-fertilization between these various foci. Because educational practice touches not only on an increasingly wide spectrum of human activities, but also because educational theory has traditionally been open to discursive influence or invasion from fields of inquiry outside of itself, it was put forward that education as a whole stands to gain to the extent that it can keep in a state of creative tension the issues that constantly adhere to those focal points.

In addition, one of the claims made in Chapter 1 for a more thorough appreciation of autobiography was that this exercise would provide a vocabulary of critique, a way of bringing to bear on individual instances of practice the concepts made available from the metalevel discussion undertaken in the present chapter. Clearly, what is beginning to emerge is a situation where it will be possible not only to evaluate in a general way the kinds of assumptions that have gone into educational projects that have come to rely on autobiography and autobiographical discourses, but also to suggest for consideration ways in which these assumptions can be tempered or tightened up, as well as to point to other areas of practice that could usefully be expanded in a particular direction. For now, these kinds of promises must be allowed to exist at the level of assertions; naturally enough, the terms of reference and points of emphasis raised in this chapter will be continually brought forward and re-introduced as our sites of inquiry in education are visited in due course.

What needs to be taken up immediately, however, and be cast in educational terms is a key idea that has been growing more insistent throughout the progress of this chapter. This is none other than the idea we found in the writings of Weintraub, Hart, Dodd, Gray, and others, that a major cultural function of autobiography is to be found in its *social* dimension. Thus within autobiography as a form of narcissistic withdrawal lies a countervailing impulse: A sense of worldliness, of social consciousness is built into the very foundations of the autobiographical urge. But what kind of educational arrangements can be made that will best foster this grounded, outward-looking, social dimension of autobiography? To what extent do the autobiographical principles and tensions discussed in this chapter complement, for example, the stated or implied goals of literacy in a democracy? These questions are large and perennially important; armed with our new conceptions of autobiography, the major portion of what is to follow in the rest of the book will be given over to more extended consideration of these and other educational issues. For now, however, as part of a wider effort to justify the use of autobiography on educational grounds, we will see how indispensable the ideas of John Dewey are for this project in literacy and the aesthetics of self-realization.

3   Dewey and the Aesthetics of Self-Realization

Except as the outcome of arrested development, there is no such thing as a fixed, readymade, finished self. Every living self causes acts and is itself caused in return by what it does. All voluntary action is a remaking of the self, since it creates new desires, instigates to new modes of endeavor, brings to light new conditions which institute new ends. Our personal identity is found in the thread of continuous development which binds together these changes. In the strictest sense, it is impossible for the self to stand still; it is becoming, and becoming for the better or the worse.

John Dewey, Ethics, *1932*

We now turn our attention away from literary theory, with its various conceptions of autobiography, toward inspecting more closely the social dimension that lies imminent within the form and begin to prepare the way for crossing from the largely theoretical and philosophical undertaking of this and the previous chapter into the world of the classroom that waits for us in the next. It is not that the tensions uncovered within the contested views of autobiography previously discussed have failed to provide us with some wider, more generous perspectives as well as with a number of fruitful and provocative ideas that may assist in grounding educational theory and practice more securely. Rather, it is that most theorizing on autobiography exists within the discursive field of literary theory and is cast primarily within those terms of reference. What remains to be discovered now is some means to translate this theory into educational terms, into educational discourse; that is, into discourse that formally addresses the world of schools, classrooms, teachers, and students. In this respect, then, while not denying the creative force of the tensions in autobiographical theory previously brought forward, some bridging maneuver is required that will ease our passage from one discursive territory to another. This chapter will argue that the materials for such a construction are to be found in the educational writings of John Dewey, and that although Dewey himself, except in rare and isolated instances, seldom alluded to or worked directly from an overt conception of autobiography, his views are, as we shall see, wholly compatible with and supportive of those notions of autobiography that have emerged to this point, and that seem to contain the most potential for education.

It ought to be mentioned here, however, that Dewey's work does more than redeem for education the social dimension of autobiography, which is by and large insufficiently stressed in literary theory. What it principally does is provide an account of experience, of inquiry, and of methods to promote reflective thinking that culminates in what I am going to call an aesthetics of self-realization. But as Dewey himself makes clear in the quotation that heads this chapter, such a conception of identity also contains an ethics of becoming, since the self, constructed as it is through a process of interaction with an environment, is always a social and ethical self, a self that if its most characteristic feature is its capacity for change, never does so in isolation, but always in relation to a community of others. It is in this sense, then, that the paradox discovered earlier in our discussion of autobiography emerges again as a prime feature of Dewey's philosophy. It was not sufficient for Dewey to say, like Socrates, that society is the individual writ large, but rather that implicated in the education of the individual, woven into the attempt to provide opportunities and moments for self-discovery and for self-knowledge, is the realization of one's connectedness to others and to society. This is what Dewey's lifelong struggle to rid our thinking of all dualisms amounted to, a belief promulgated in the first article of *My Pedagogic Creed* (1929): "All education proceeds by the participation of the individual in the social consciousness of the race" (p. 3). But this is to anticipate somewhat.

The larger, more comprehensive objectives of this chapter must take into account in a more systematic way those fundamental aspects of Dewey's thinking that are required to sustain the argument that Dewey is an essential and indispensable figure in providing a source of educational and philosophical warrants for our work in autobiography. To accomplish this, we could do no better than to follow, briefly at some moments, in more depth at others, the emergence and development of some major elements in Dewey's philosophy, aware at all times not only of how they illuminate the educational importance of autobiography, but also of how they may be pressed into service as the bridge between the discursive fields of literary theory and educational theory and practice. Specifically, this chapter will pursue the following organizational scheme.

First, I will discuss Dewey's period of tenure at the University of Chicago from 1894–1904, a period that saw not only the establishment of the Laboratory School in which, for example, Dewey's friend George Herbert Mead taught and conducted experiments, but, more importantly for our purpose here, was the period in which Dewey wrote such seminal works as *The School and Society* (1900/1967) and *The Child and the Curriculum* (1902/1963). As we will discover, Dewey owed many of his ideas on the social construction of the self to Mead, a fact he freely acknowledged on a number of occasions (see Rucker, 1969, p. 59). Contained in embryo in his writings from this formative stage in his career are many of the key themes he both elaborated on and defended for the rest of his long life, ideas such as his suspicion of all dualistic thinking and his insistence on a fully developed theory of experience and key concepts like instrumentalism and reconstruction, as well as a bold conception of inquiry. Most of these will be introduced and discussed in the first sections of the chapter in order to prepare the ground for an understanding of how Dewey built his more mature philosophy upon these particular foundations.

Second, I will inspect the work Dewey produced while at Columbia University from 1904 to roughly 1925, a period that ended with the publication of *Experience and Nature* (1925/1958). In particular, attention will be given to reviewing the principles of reflective thinking that were adumbrated in earlier works but found fuller expression in *How We Think* (1910/1933), a work written especially for teachers and educators. As well, although considerations of space prohibit the kind of treatment the work so clearly warrants, some time will be spent on Dewey's *Democracy and Education* (1916/1964), especially those parts that deal with his theory of experience. This is undertaken as preparatory to a more extended discussion of aesthetic experience that emerges from the latter stages of his career.

Third, then, the main aspects of a masterwork from his retirement years, *Art as Experience* (1934/1980), will draw our inspection of Dewey's thinking to a close. Fittingly enough for one who believed so thoroughly in the idea of life as a process of continuous growth, this biographical and developmental approach to Dewey's work will culminate in a recapitulation of the main details of his achievement insofar as they highlight and suggest themselves as essential for justifying the educational deployment of autobiography that is our primary focus. It is of interest to note in this connection that the interpretation and discussion entered into throughout the remainder of this chapter not only serves the narrow aim of our particular concerns with autobiography, but also may legitimately be extended to demonstrate to educators that a measure of injustice has been done to Dewey's work by those who hold him responsible for some of the excesses of the progressive education movement. Although we shall have to wait until the concluding chapter to argue more precisely for the importance and place of autobiography in a contemporary approach to literacy called "whole language" as an aspect of the rising paradigm within language arts education that travels under the sobriquet of the New Literacy (Willinsky, 1990b), it is important that we reserve a place for Dewey's work in advance. For if Dewey himself and the ideas he so painstakingly promoted have in many ways been affected negatively by the growth of what Bernstein (1960) calls "the Dewey legend" (p. ix), it will become clear, at least tacitly for now, that the power and relevance of Dewey's thinking in both its psychological and philosophical coloration were not laid to rest with the demise of the progressive education movement (Cremin, 1961), but that it lives on as an informing principle, a powerful ideological support for educators in many school subjects for whom process is more important than product, self-understanding more sought after than ephemeral acquaintance with facts.

With this brief introduction as a backdrop, we pass now to a consideration of Dewey's work and its relation to the educational value of autobiography.

DEWEY AT CHICAGO: FROM ABSOLUTISM TO EXPERIMENTALISM

In his lucid account of the birth and gestation of the school of philosophy established at the new University of Chicago in 1894, Rucker takes great care to show that although it could be argued that John Dewey was the driving force behind the formation of what was perceived as a new system of philosophy, this new system was in fact the result of the fortuitous meeting of a number of brilliant and distinguished minds. Indeed, no less a figure than William James gave public recognition of the communal nature of the "Chicago School's" achievements when he wrote that "Professor John Dewey, and at least ten of his disciples, have collectively put into the world a statement, homogeneous in spite of so many cooperating minds, of a view of the world both theoretical and practical" (cited in Rucker, 1969, pp. 3–4). However, although the new university itself was generously supported by John D. Rockefeller to the tune of $35 million over a 15-year period, which allowed university president Harper the luxury of handpicking the staff he wanted, no one could have predicted the extent to which the intellectual interests of a substantial number of the faculty in the departments of philosophy, psychology, and pedagogy would combine and dovetail in quite the manner they did. We need, therefore, to ask what worldview it was that excited James to wax so eloquently in praise of Dewey and his colleagues.

The simple but unsatisfactory answer is that it was the philosophy of pragmatism that united these men from several distinct disciplines. Simple, because it was indeed a form of pragmatism that they subscribed to, a form that stood closer to James's own "pragmaticism," with its belief in the practical nature of all knowledge, than to the pragmatism of C. S. Pierce. But unsatisfactory, since pragmatism itself as a philosophy had even by then been tarred with the brush of espousing a shortsighted belief in expediency, of worshipping whatever works. Although ultimately, perhaps, there is still little chance of shaking pragmatism free from some of its less appealing connotations, it is necessary that we become more clear over those features that set this philosophy apart and that provided the worldview that claimed the support of Dewey and so many of his followers.

Dewey himself, in his autobiographical essay "From Absolutism to Experimentalism" (1960a), in which he reflected on the men and ideas that influenced his intellectual development, provides a starting point from which we can progress toward a more accurate account. For the young Dewey, what initially attracted him to Hegelianism was less the technicalities of the dialectic, although the Hegelian synthesis did operate "as an immense release, a liberation" (Dewey, 1960a, p. 10), but rather the manner in which Hegel elevated the organic into a philosophic category. As Bernstein (1960) states in his comment on the fascination of the organic for Dewey:

> An organic unity is a whole in which there is differentiation without segmentation, for the distinctions within it are functional in character. The category also focuses attention on the necessity of understanding the genesis and development of an idea in order to know its nature. And finally, only the organic adequately represents experience in its specificity and concreteness. (p. xxi)

The category of the organic derived from Hegel persisted with Dewey throughout his career. It can be seen everywhere in his view of experience as an interaction between an organism and its environment, to the extent that if we neglect the contextual nature of all experiences we similarly fail to appreciate their organic character. In addition to Hegel, Dewey was heavily influenced by Darwin's theory of evolution, but from a more subtle standpoint than was espoused by the social Darwinists. For Dewey, Darwin's work showed that man could be studied scientifically as a biological creature; this biological approach also turned up for Dewey in the work of William James himself, which for Dewey "led straight to the perception of the importance of distinctive social categories, especially communication and participation" (Dewey, 1960a, p. 17). It was this biological perspective, from which experience was viewed as an active process with psychological, ethical, and social consequences, that helped to undergird the new system of philosophy at Chicago and that provided the grounds for its worldview.

But the biological notion of organic process allows for more than this, since in Darwinian, evolutionary terms all behavior is purposive, teleological. This biological function involves growth, forward movement, a process in which the end of experience, its *telos*, is always changing, always tentative, as the activity itself progresses. This would account for the frequency with which Dewey was fond of quoting, for example in *Art as Experience* (1934/1980, p. 193) and *Experience and Education* (1938, p. 35), the familiar lines from Tennyson's "Ulysses":

> Yet all experience is an arch wherethro'
> Gleams that untraveled world, whose margin fades
> For ever and for ever when I move. (19–21)

However else we might wish to interpret this Ulyssean project, in Deweyan terms it signifies a neverending process of self-construction, an ongoing and continuous interaction in which a willing, purposive subject conditions and is conditioned by the changing nature of the particular, proximate end. The worldview that emerges from these foundations contains three important features, which may be summarized as follows.

First, the Chicago view of pragmatism conceives it as a theory of process based on a notion of activity in which both people and objects are a result of the process. Second, mind or consciousness itself is a social product brought about through the continuous interaction of free agents. And third, all ends are provisional, changing; it is a process that allows, as in classic evolutionary terms, for novelty, and one that invalidates the idea of fixed goals.

Epistemologically, these principles square with a conception of knowledge and knowledge creation that places the emphasis on its constructed, unfixed, and provisional nature. In this instance, knowledge is not something "out there," objective, eternal, waiting to be discovered, but is rather to be found by means of those tools or instruments that are of man's own devising. This epistemological standpoint has crucial repercussions for education and especially for the possibilities of self-knowledge, a major component of the autobiographical impulse itself. Nor did these consequences escape either Dewey or his colleague Mead; indeed, the closeness of their thinking on the application of these principles to the field of education is indicated by the fact that Mead and his wife edited Dewey's 1899 lectures for publication under the title *The School and Society* (1900/1967). In this work we can find the clearest expression of Dewey's application of the working hypotheses derived from the specifics of his earlier thinking, and it is to a consideration of these hypotheses that we now turn.

In the early chapters of *The School and Society,* Dewey argues for a fresh approach to contemporary conceptions of the school and the child, largely based on his contention, formalized later in Article II of *My Pedagogic Creed* (1929), that "education . . . is a process of living and not a preparation for future living" (p. 6). With this axiom Dewey took aim at an education system that for him lacked not only vitality, but also failed to engage the student in any meaningful way by linking the student's own experience outside the school with that which took place inside the school. For Dewey, contemporary conceptions of knowledge and schooling labored under a Lockean empiricism with its view of the mind as passive, a blank slate; instruction in this case involved large doses of memory work at the same time as it paid little heed to the kind of knowledges students already possessed and brought with them to school. In this book Dewey not only provided charts and diagrams that attempted to show in physical terms what these new schools and classrooms would look like, but he also argued for an active role for education in the promotion of social progress. Here he tried to show that the school was a kind of dinosaur, doomed to extinction in its present form because it had failed to adapt to the rapid pace with which American society itself was evolving. For Dewey (1900/1967), "Knowledge itself is no longer an immobile solid; it has been liquified. It is actively moving in all the currents of society itself" (p. 25). This prototypically modernist idea, described recently by Berman (1988) as "a struggle to make ourselves at home in a constantly changing world" (p. 6), spelled, for Dewey, a radical moment out of which a myriad of possibilities for human growth could emerge. A large part of the reason for the resistance within education to these possibilities Dewey laid at the feet of an outmoded psychology, and in a memorable chapter in the latter half of the book entitled "The Psychology of Elementary Education," he contrasts his own psychological principles with "the psychology of former days" (Dewey, 1900/1967, p. 98).

Under the old psychology, states Dewey (1900/1967), mind was a purely individual affair "in direct naked contact with an external world" (p. 98). Under the new psychology, mind is "a function of social life . . . requiring continual stimulus from social agencies, and finding its nutrition in social supplies" (p. 99). Previously it was thought that the child's mind was supposed to be filled by direct contact with the world, embodied in traditional subjects like geography or arithmetic. What had been overlooked was the fact that these subjects themselves "were simply selections from the social life of the past" (p. 100), and that because this social element was missing, the subject matter itself exerted little intrinsic appeal for students. Such learning that took place was wholly due to the "encouragements, admonitions, urgings and devices of the instructor" (p. 100), but it was distinctively empty of any appeal to the child's present needs and aims, needs that in practice Dewey saw as largely social.

Second, the old psychology as a psychology of knowledge and intellect made "Facts, laws [and] information . . . the staple of the curriculum" (p. 101) to the exclusion of any consideration of emotion. This separation of affect from cognition resulted in a dualism under which no attempt was made to connect the life of the mind with "the problems and interests of the life of practice" (p. 102). And finally, in a recapitulation of a cornerstone in pragmatic thinking, mind is essentially "a process of growth, not a fixed thing" (p. 102). Before, the child's mind had been conceived as a scaled-down version of the adult's, with faculties that, like muscles, required continuous exercise to ensure their development. For Dewey, the growth of a child's mind is a changing affair, one that presents "phases of capacity and interest" (p. 102) at different developmental periods. To ignore this is to force-feed the child when he or she may have neither the capacity nor the interest to engage readily with the subject matter.

Although Dewey (1900/1967) does proceed to offer (pp. 105–111) cogent observations on the relation of subject matter to the stages of growth in the child, he devotes considerable space to remarking on one of the most important means for "extending and controlling experience" (p. 111), namely, the child's command of the symbol systems of language and number. Language and number "represent the tools which society has evolved in the past as the instruments of its intellectual pursuits. They represent the keys which will unlock to the child the wealth of social capital which lies beyond the possible range of his limited individual experience" (p. 111). And it is with extending, deepening, and making more coherent the specifics of the child's individual experience by means of language that Dewey is largely concerned. For, as he later goes on to expound in the short but passionately argued *The Child and the Curriculum* (1902/1963), by viewing the child as "the starting point, the center, and the end" (p. 9), by introducing the child's experience into the classroom as the prime focus of attention, language itself in both spoken and written form can function as a privileged instrument by means of which the child's growth can be fostered. And in a telling and significant assertion Dewey states: "Personality, character, is more than subject-matter. Not knowledge or information, but self-realization is the goal. To possess all the world of knowledge and lose one's self is as awful a fate in education as in religion" (1902/1963, p. 9).

In his effort, then, to dissolve what he clearly feels is a false and pernicious opposition between the child and the curriculum (or as he dramatically frames it, the child versus the curriculum), Dewey recommends that we place all our educational cards on the side of the child's growth and self-realization. This project of self-realization owes little to Rousseau's notion of negative education whereby the growing Emile was kept blissfully free from the dubious fruits of self-consciousness, but is rather motivated and problematized by Mead's (1959) guiding question, "How can an individual get outside of himself (experientially) in such a way as to become an object to himself?" (p. 215). For let there be no mistake: in the matter of creating the conditions whereby the problem of selfhood or self-consciousness can best be addressed, Mead and Dewey are of one mind. So it is, then, that part of a solution to this problem is to be discovered "by referring to the process of social conduct or activity in which the given person or individual is implicated" (Mead, 1959, p. 215). And as a site that by its very nature is a place set apart and sanctioned by society for the acculturation and socialization of the child, the school would seem to suggest itself as ideal for promoting such an end. For Mead and for Dewey, rationality and intelligence itself begin in the crucial moment when an individual starts to take an objective, impersonal attitude to himself and to his experience.

In the same way that mind is socially constructed, "The self, as that which can be an object to itself, is essentially a social structure, and it arises in social experience" (Mead, 1959, p. 217). By responding to oneself as another might respond to oneself, by developing what Vygotsky (1962) was later to call "inner speech," the individual initiates "a conversation of gestures with himself" (p. 218). This kind of thinking, this mode of reflection, is a necessary part of preparing oneself for social action. On this score Mead is here worth quoting at length:

> One separates the significance of what he is saying to others from the actual speech and gets it ready before saying it. He thinks it out, and perhaps writes it in the form of a book; but it is still a part of social intercourse in which one is addressing other persons and at the same time addressing oneself. . . . I know of no other form of behavior than the linguistic in which the individual is an object to himself, and, so far as I can see, the individual is not a self in the reflexive sense unless he is an object to himself. (Mead, 1959, p. 219)

Mead's concept of the "generalized other" states that our fullest selfhood cannot be achieved until we are capable not only of taking the attitudes of others toward ourselves and making them part of our experience, but also of internalizing their understanding of the commonly held beliefs developed as part of a social group. Consequently, what emerges from Mead's work as a logical adjunct to Dewey's ideas on the ultimate purpose of education is the key contention that it is at bottom the social groups or communities to which we belong that ultimately create the conditions under which our selves may develop and the possibilities for self-realization be achieved. Self-consciousness, according to Mead (1959), provides the primary structure of the self and is "thus essentially a cognitive rather than an emotional phenomenon" (p. 241). If this is so, then the origin of the self is to be discovered in that inner conversation which constitutes thinking and in which reflection proceeds. And as both Dewey and Mead would have it, this self is therefore, in all respects, social.

The arguments of Dewey's earlier, popular, and more accessible works, as well as moments in Mead's thinking on the social nature of the self, have been offered here as crucial examples of the kind of warrants required to argue for the value of autobiography in education, a value that, it is held, comes closest to embodying in its purest form the major educational goal of self-realization, a goal that Dewey argued was the sine qua non of a truly child-centered approach. Certainly I am alive to the objection that autobiography under other views of education may not be accorded so privileged a position, a fact that will be confirmed in the next chapter to temper any tendency

to overstate the case. Nevertheless, as we move now to a consideration of some aspects of Dewey's work from his period at Columbia
University, especially his views of experience and reflective thinking,
we will begin to extend our appreciation not only of the extent to
which Dewey's work takes up many of the themes introduced earlier,
but of how, with the goal of self-realization before us, the narrative
potential within autobiography itself can be justified and recommended as a primary instrument of thought. Moreover, if Bruner
(1979) is correct that "It is often the case that development of the general idea comes from a first round of experience with concrete em-
bodiments of ideas that are close to a child's life" (p. 123), then Dewey's method for promoting reflective thinking (which is also a theory
of inquiry) can be combined in the autobiographical act with Mead's
contention that we must somehow get outside of ourselves and in
that movement and moment embark on the continuous activity of
self-discovery.

DEWEY AT COLUMBIA:
A VIEW OF EXPERIENCE,
THE CONSEQUENCES OF INQUIRY

In 1904, when University of Chicago president Harper notified
Dewey that Mrs. Dewey's appointment as principal of the Laboratory
School would not be renewed, this event among others, including a
longstanding feud between Dewey and the dean of education, Wilbur
S. Jackson, convinced Dewey that he could no longer remain in Chicago. Dewey's resignation, while not entirely unexpected, did mean
that America's foremost living philosopher was in the market for a
new position from which to carry forward the important work begun
at Chicago. Such a post was not long in materializing, and in 1904
Dewey began his period of tenure at Columbia University and Teachers College, a period that saw the publication of his most considered
and finest statement on education, *Democracy and Education* (1916/
1964). Already, however, some of the more dramatic features of the
Laboratory School's educational experiments, such as the stimulation
of the child's interest in relation to the life of the child outside school,
had led to a caricature of the "Dewey method" as one that simply
turned students loose to follow their own passing interests without
the intelligent guidance of a teacher. But if closer attention had been
paid even to Dewey's more popular works like *The School and Society*
and *The Child and the Curriculum*, then it would have been apparent

that such a notion ran counter to the fundamental principles of psychology and social theory that those works contained.

As we saw then in our discussion and will pursue in this section in more detail, experience of the past provides a fund on which we can draw at any time; but this funded experience is only truly available to the child as he or she is guided within a social process that attempts to develop the mental tools and habits necessary to utilize that fund. The reason for stimulating the child to discover a problem of his or her own, one that is not artificially derived from textbooks or the interests of the teacher, is for the sake of fostering "discipline, or gain in power of control; that is a *habit* of considering problems" (Dewey, 1900/1967, p. 149, emphasis in original). And as Dewey (1900/1967) goes on to assert, "So completely have the conditions for securing this self-putting of problems been neglected that the very idea of voluntary attention has been radically perverted" (p. 149). One of the cardinal functions of the teacher, then, is to assist in stimulating and guiding the pursuit of true reflective attention, attention that is self-directed and involves the child in the use of judgment, reason, and deliberation. In other words, the teacher as well as the student must be put in possession of principles of reflective thinking that represent not only a theory of inquiry but also a way of securing knowledge through the development of personal insight into a felt problem.

In this way, and consistent with the view of education put forward in *My Pedagogic Creed*, education is a continuous reconstruction of experience in the light of the past and of problems arising in the present. The value of this reconstruction is measured against its effect on the extent to which it creates in the child those habits and predispositions that are receptive to the assimilation of further experiences that may be added to that growing fund. These two issues, the analysis of reflective experience and the difficulties of valuation, occupied Dewey for much of the first two decades of the twentieth century. Although it was not until much later that Dewey tried to pursue, and only then in a tantalizingly oblique and understated manner, the likely consequences for self-realization when his own principles of reflection were combined with Mead's theory of the social construction of the self, his work on the nature of reflective experience is essential for our burgeoning conceptions of autobiography. As this discussion unfolds it will become easier to discern how the autobiographical urge toward reconstructing one's life experiences, whether in narrative or in some other medium, and with all the attendant problems and possibilities discussed in the previous chapter, is compatible with the principles of reflection and experience advanced by Dewey himself.

Dewey on Experience and Thinking

I have chosen to discuss, first of all, Dewey's comments on the nature of experience and reflection that he advances in *Democracy and Education* (1916/1964), rather than proceed in chronological fashion by considering the principles of inquiry set forth in his earlier book for teachers, *How We Think* (1910/1933). In this way the full impact of our argument for the use of narrative as an instrument of inquiry or reflection suitable for reconstructing the qualitative aspects of past experience will emerge as a consequence of Dewey's method for going to work on those experiences. Consequently, we require for now in abbreviated form some notion of Dewey's conception of experience as a preface to discussing his principles of inquiry more fully.

For Dewey (1916/1964), experience can only be understood if we take note that "it includes an active and a passive element peculiarly combined" (p. 139). The active element is contained in seeing experience as trying something (a term Dewey links to the idea of an experiment), while the passive element connotes the idea of undergoing. In brief, what this means is that when we experience something, we do something, and then "we suffer or undergo the consequences" (p. 139). If we leave to one side for the moment the objection unaddressed by Dewey that to undergo something is also to be to some degree actively involved in shaping the nature of that experience, Dewey (1916/1964) claims that "when the change made by action is reflected back into a change made in us, the mere flux is loaded with significance. We learn something" (p. 139). However, simply moving on from one so-called experience to another is not what Dewey has in mind by his idea of experience. If we are indeed to learn from experience, there must be a sense of cumulative growth, a sense in which the meaning of an experience is contained in its capacity to cause us to predict or foresee what could happen next, hence contributing to our feeling of control. Under these conditions our actions become "an experiment with the world to find out what it is like" (p. 140), while the undergoing becomes instruction, "discovery of the connection of things" (p. 140).

The consequences for education of this view of experience are, according to Dewey (1916/1964), twofold: experience as an active-passive affair "is not primarily cognitive" (p. 140), and the value of an experience resides in the "perception of relationships or continuities to which it leads up" (p. 140). No longer can the appropriation of knowledge be conceived of as the direct application of intellectual energy (and here yet again Dewey seems to work from a very narrow conception of action), since this would sever mind or consciousness from "the physical organs of activity" (p. 140). Rather, this mind-body dualism has been the cause of the "evil results" (p. 141) of suppressing the student's bodily activities in order to better focus the mind on the material. Under this scenario there is a premium put on silence in the classroom, on discipline, and on conformity by the students to these procedural rules.

In addition, this mind-body separation places "an emphasis on *things* at the expense of *relations* or connections" (p. 143, emphasis in original). For Dewey, the view that the mind perceives things apart from their relations to other things is a pernicious half-truth that emphasizes only the isolated qualities of an object, a table, say, or a chair, rather than connecting it with other notions such as "the purpose which makes it a chair . . . or the 'period' which it represents" (p. 143). Hunting for connections, discerning the way in which things are interrelated, constitutes the intellectual and hence educative aspects of a genuine experience.

In this instance, then, it is impossible to have a meaningful experience in Dewey's view without some element of thought taking place. Seeking to supply the missing links, by attempting to discover connections in our experience, is to engage in reflective thinking, a process that also changes the quality of the experience at the same time as that experience is given a meaning that it may not have possessed in isolation. Thinking "is the intellectual endeavor to discover specific connections between something which we do and the consequences which result, so that the two become continuous" (Dewey, 1916/1964, p. 145). Although we will consider what Dewey came to call the experiential continuum in another context in the following section, it is important here to note two consequences of Dewey's ideas that bear heavily on the relationship we would make between reflective experience and autobiography.

First, if reflection involves pointing out the unities and connections within experience, then as such it could be construed in a conservative manner as an argument for maintaining the status quo, for saying in effect that because events have emerged the way they are at this moment, then they ought to continue in this way, since to disturb them would be to destroy that continuous sense of myself as a unit. To cling to this argument, however, would be to seriously misunderstand the thrust of Dewey's ideas. For Dewey, the starting point of any process of thinking is something going on, something that, as he states, "is incomplete and unfulfilled" (1916/1964, p. 146). The point or meaning of reflection is not simply to arrive at an awareness of what is the case, what at this moment bears on the present situation. Rather, "its meaning lies literally in what is *going* to be, in how it is *going* to turn out" (p. 146, emphasis added). To think is therefore to begin to develop "an identification with our own destiny" (p. 147), to develop a responsibility for the kinds of consequences that will inevitably flow from our next attempt, our next experiment with reality. In this way reflection becomes the springboard for further action.

Second, to hold that thinking takes place with reference to something that is still going on is to say that uncertainty is woven into the very fabric of the process. As such, the object of thinking is to assist in reaching a conclusion, however tentative, that will provide the terms of reference for our next movement forward. If thinking "is a process of inquiry, of looking into things, of investigating" (1916/1964, p. 148), then it is by its very nature tentative. Etymologically, according to the OED, tentative means "experimental; done as a trial"; hence there is a real way in which thinking is always provisional, always in search of the next series of qualifications. It is this sense of the provisional that Dewey (1916/1964) wants to claim is the characteristic of all active thinking, a situation in which these "tentative inferences will take effect in *a* method of procedure appropriate to *his* situation" (p. 149, emphasis in original). And as we will witness immediately, although Dewey's principles of inquiry appear on the surface, and indeed were taken to be at the time, paradigmatic of the general process of scientific method, it is clear from the foregoing discussion that they certainly do not rule out the possibility of other methods or procedures for thinking, procedures which, like narrative, are entirely appropriate as instruments of reflection whose main object in this instance is the furtherance of self-knowledge, of self-realization.

Dewey on Inquiry-as-Reflection

If one were to search for a statement that performed the function of encapsulating the essence of Dewey's approach to education that emerged from combining his own thinking with the experimental data gleaned from the Chicago Laboratory School, one would find it contained in Dewey's preface to the first edition of his book for educators, *How We Think* (1910/1933). As we shall see, Dewey might with equal accuracy have named the book "Why We Think," since he is overwhelmingly concerned with developing an awareness of the purpose of reflective thinking, even as he argues for how we are actually to go about that process. Thus, in the first paragraph of his preface, Dewey advances his views on method, on the nature of the child, and on the intended outcome of the process of inquiry, statements that fairly capture the essence of his beliefs.

For Dewey (1910/1933), his book represents his conviction that some principle, or as he terms it, some "steadying and centralizing factor" (p. v), must be found to bring a sense of unity to a pedagogical situation that has become fragmented owing to the multiplication of tasks and demands on a teacher's time and abilities. Dewey finds this steadying factor by recommending that teachers adopt "that attitude of mind, that habit of thought" (p. v) that is called scientific. He wants to defend this recommendation against the charge that the scientific attitude of mind is irrelevant to teaching young people by a psychological appeal to the nature of the child, since this eponymous being is marked by "ardent curiosity and fertile imagination" (p. v), attitudes that come very near to the scientific attitude itself. The outcome of adopting this process of inquiry is expressed in the utilitarian language of the progressive reformers among whom Dewey was, for a time, a leading spokesman. By claiming that the consequences for educational practice would make "for individual happiness and the reduction of social waste" (p. v), Dewey was recapitulating two of the most important planks in the progressives' broad platform for education. Dewey's book, then, and the principles of reflective thinking for which he argues, must be seen as part of a larger social and educational mission directed not only at improving instruction, but at fostering the kinds of habits in children that it was believed would provide one of the best chances for the long-term development of social progress.

Based on the notion that reflection is "not simply a sequence of ideas, but a *con*-sequence" (Dewey, 1910/1933, p. 4, emphasis in original), where "each [idea] determines the next as its proper outcome, while each outcome in turn leans back on, or refers to, its predecessors" (p. 4), Dewey is anxious to assert the proposition that thinking "is practically synonymous with believing" (p. 6). Reflective thinking, then, is offered as an antidote and alternative to the view of the genesis of that sort of belief which we call prejudice, that is, prejudgments, "not conclusions reached as the result of personal mental activity" (p. 7) but unexamined ideas randomly extracted from a general body of ideas that are currently "in the air." To offer the principles of reflective thinking was to attempt to combat the forces of inertia, custom, and laziness that Dewey felt were endemic within society at large and that had found a breeding ground in the schools through views and practices that stressed a narrow, empiricist view of knowledge, with the consequent creation of a docile and disinterested student body. Reflective thought as the "active, persistent, and careful consideration of any belief or supposed form of knowledge in the light of the grounds that support it and the further conclusions to which it tends" (p. 9) promotes a view of knowledge as warranted belief, a state itself, however, that, owing to the interactive nature of the very process of inquiry, renders knowledge temporary, constitutive of that principle of radical uncertainty that we witnessed earlier as a feature of Dewey's conception of experience itself.

As Dewey (1910/1933) summarizes them, there are five logical moments within a reflective experience:

> (i) a felt difficulty; (ii) its location and definition; (iii) suggestions of possible solution; (iv) development by reason of the bearings of the suggestions; (v) further observations and experiment leading to its acceptance or rejection; that is the conclusion of belief or disbelief. (p. 72)

In this view reflective thinking always involves some disruption in the flow of experience; some portion of experience is isolated as the "given" of the situation, the difficulty that constitutes "the problem." If we then proceed on the premise that the meanings found on the location of the problem suggest going beyond what is immediately present to risk coming up with an illuminating hypothesis, then our deliberations on the hypothesis may lead us to devise a method of testing it. Finally, on the basis of the kinds of instruments we construct for testing the hypothesis rests the acceptance or rejection of the hypothesis, that is, it leads to a situation in which our beliefs are warranted or not. Stated in this way, the logic of these principles is indeed indicative of a view of inquiry and its in-the-flesh avatar self-the-scientist: an active, open, hypothesis-testing individual. Naturally enough, no person proceeds in isolation; this fact accounts for the notion that because there already exist instruments for testing our hypotheses developed over time from the funded experience of a community of individuals, there is certainly more than one type of inquiry, types motivated by more than wanting to simply test the features of the external, physical world. As Bernstein (1960) cogently puts it: "Dewey, like Aristotle, realized that different subject-matters require different rules of procedure, and the various types of inquiry will have differing degrees of precision" (p. xxxi). Thus truth criteria themselves develop from, and are a function of, the various instruments devised within separate fields of inquiry to test whether our belief in a certain hypothesis is reasonable or not. Dewey's point, of course, would be that the method or instrument through which we gain knowledge and justify it is exactly what gives it its cognitive status. In other words, the constructivist view supports the idea that knowledge itself is a function of the instruments man has devised for exploring his environment.

Now it might be argued that this view of reflective thinking, of the principles of inquiry, is all very well for more overtly scientific undertakings like chemistry or physics, but that it works less well when "the problem" or object of attention is our own experience, the facts of our biographies. In this instance, qualitative, aesthetic considerations come into play that set them apart from other modes of experience and for which scientific procedures of inquiry with their instruments for thinking are inappropriate or less applicable. It is precisely this objection that prompted Bruner (1986), a contemporary constructivist himself in the Deweyan mold, to assert that there are indeed but two modes of cognitive functioning, "two modes of thought, each providing distinctive ways of ordering experience, of constructing reality" (p. 11). One mode, of course, is the well-formed argument that is analogous here to scientific methods for establishing formal, empirical proof. The other mode is narrative, the constituent of a "good story" (p. 11). Arguments are designed to convince because of their truth, but the other mode (narrative) "establishes not truth but verisimilitude" (p. 11). The "goodness" of a story is then to be judged, on this constructivist view of thought, by criteria derived from the practice of literary interpretation rather than on criteria used to judge the adequacy of an argument or a scientific proof. Clearly Bruner's own argument, although saying nothing about other mediums that might also wish to claim similar cognitive status (cf. Eisner, 1982), is not only a gloss on what one might be entitled to deduce from an examination of Dewey's notion of reflective thinking (with which Bruner is undoubtedly familiar), but is also consistent with Dewey's point that the instruments of thought are domain specific and we ought not to judge their effectiveness wholly on the degrees of precision they allow, but rather as they facilitate or inhibit the possibility of future inquiry.

And it is not only with narrative in mind, but with other mediums of artistic representation for rendering the peculiar qualities of human experience as well, that we turn to our examination of the culminating stages of Dewey's work.

DEWEY AND THE AESTHETICS OF SELF-REALIZATION

In the winter and spring of 1931, Dewey was invited by the philosophy department at Harvard University to deliver the William James memorial lecture series. His chosen topic was the philosophy of art, on the face of it a topic that did not seem to spring immediately from the bulk of Dewey's published work at that time. But as we shall see, the topic of art as experience represented in many ways a culmination, or as Dewey would have it, a consummation of his thinking on the nature of experience. As always, it seemed, Dewey had spied a situation of discontinuity, a dualism, a breach that required a healing touch which would restore a sense of unity and wholeness to that situation. In this case the dualism was the perceived rift between art and ordinary experience, in that, for Dewey, aesthetic theory had become an obstruction to the perception and appreciation of works of art themselves, since the art object had become "separated from both conditions of origin and operation in experience" (Dewey, 1934/1980, p. 3). To build a wall around the art object as aesthetic theory tended to do was, for Dewey, to commit art to a separate realm and to cut it off from its rightful place as part of human effort and achievement. It was, in other words, to mystify art by banishing it from contact with the material facts of its production and consumption, and from conditions under which it might move and have an effect on the world. Dewey's (1934/1980) task, then, was, in his own words, "to restore continuity between the refined and intensified forms of experience that are works of art and the everyday events, doings, and sufferings that are universally recognized to constitute experience" (p. 3).

But as I will go on to argue now, Dewey's self-imposed excursion into aesthetics is not simply for the benefit of that field of inquiry alone; it is much more than that, and may best be seen as a considered and fitting climax to the kind of thinking we have been discussing thus far. Before inspecting his work on aesthetic experience more closely, and in particular his comments on the ways in which we can give it form and shape, I want briefly to outline the argument I will pursue here, to which the subsequent examples from Dewey's work on the natural history of form will constitute the source of the evidence required to support these claims.

The link between Dewey's general theory of experience expounded earlier and his views on art is to see them as, in fact, parts of a whole. An experience is an experience for Dewey only when it fulfills two cardinal criteria: (1) that it "takes up something from those which have gone before and modifies in some way those which come after" (Dewey, 1938, p. 35), a clear statement of Dewey's principle of the experiential continuum; and (2) when there is the possibility that "the material experienced runs its course to fulfillment" (Dewey, 1934/ 1980, p. 35). In this latter case, fulfillment connotes the conception of an experience that is satisfactory, such as finding the solution to a problem, eating a meal, playing a game. In Dewey's (1934/1980) words, the experience is "so rounded out that its close is a consummation and not a cessation" (p. 35). When we take into consideration all that has been said before regarding the constant interaction between an organism and its environment, with all the change, discontinuity, and incompleteness that this implies, the possibilities for human fulfillment and self-realization lie in the extent of its successful integration with the surrounding conditions. Aesthetic experience is nothing less than the integration that heals the disorientations and disturbances which everyone is heir to in the process of living. Consequently, aesthetic experience expands and enriches our lives and can be achieved, as Dewey had earlier stated in *Experience and Nature* (1925/1958), by "acts of all kinds that directly refresh and enlarge the spirit and that are instrumental to the production of new objects and dispositions" (p. 365). In addition, the pervasive quality of aesthetic experience is also instrumental in providing the likelihood of unity within and among experiences. Since for Dewey (1934/1980) life displays no uniformity but is rather "a thing of histories, each with its own plot, its own inception and movement towards its close" (p. 36), it is the dominant quality of the experience that remains in the mind after the experience that supplies its integrative force in spite of the range of variations of its separate parts. Implicit, then, within every experience that is an experience is this qualitative, consummatory aspect that conduces to a sense of wholeness. Thus, any experience may contain the possibility of its being considered aesthetic; the point here is that we are speaking now of degrees rather than kinds of experience. However, from this outline we are able to sustain the assertion that it is aesthetic experience itself that is constitutive of an individual's self-realization.

This argument has immediate consequences for education at large as well as for the place and function of autobiography within it, which is the principal and abiding focus of our concern throughout. But if the argument persuades in one sense, in another sense it may be held to lack some indication of what gives form or shape to an aesthetic experience, since if a consummating experience is one that is rounded out, brought to a satisfactory close rather than simply abandoned *in medias res*, then we may legitimately request some notion of form, since the autobiographical act itself presupposes a concern for the manner in which past experience is shaped and ordered. And it is with Dewey's thoughts on form that we bring this final section to a close.

First, it is important to note that, for Dewey, form is not an exclusive property of objects that we name works of art. There is, he claims, an "inevitable tendency" (Dewey, 1934/1980, p. 137) for human beings to wish to so order events that they take on a complete and unified character. In saying this, Dewey wants to hold that form is an integral part of any experience that is, by his definition, an experience. The tendency toward order and shapeliness that we find in art is only a more obvious example of a general tendency within human experience itself. Form, then, is defined by Dewey (1934/1980) "as the operation of forces that carry the experience of an event, object, scene, and situation to its own integral fulfillment" (p. 137). In its function as a carrier of meaning, form is therefore implied or inherent in the very nature of the substance or content, not something that is imposed from without. In other words, fourteen lines of iambic pentameter with a fixed rhyme scheme, or a dramatic monologue, or a three-act play, are appropriate in order to carry forward only certain kinds of subject matter to fulfillment; the artistic problem, therefore, concerns the discovery and deployment of the form by means of which the consummating close may be effected.

Second, there can be no possibility of this movement toward consummation unless "there is a progressive massing of values, a cumulative effect" (Dewey, 1934/1980, p. 137). Here, the importance of the experiential continuum is seen to greatest effect, in that to provide for the sense of continuity, of formal movement, the accumulated experience must be selected in order to create "suspense and anticipation of resolution" (p. 137). This would tend to explain our fascination with examining the preliminary sketches for a painting, the successive drafts of a poem, the changing time signatures and phrasing of a musical composition, as our concern for the *process* of artistic creation, one that seeks to lend currency to the notion that the completed object did not occur in a once-and-for-all manner at a given point, but is itself the product of a whole chain of minor (and sometimes major) consummatory moments.

Third, even when such characteristics as continuity and anticipation are built into our ideas of aesthetic form, we must also take into account "the factor of resistance" (p. 138), without which there would be no sense of development or fulfillment, but under which the act would be "a fluid rush to a straightaway mark" (p. 138). Resistance, in the form of tension or difficulties that have to be overcome in order to unify and bring the experience to a consummatory moment, highlights "the place of intelligence" (p. 138) in the production of the art object and is analogous to the application of those principles of inquiry or reflection over which we earlier spent some time. But for the artist the problem is more immediate than for the scientist, since as Dewey (1934/1980) notes, "to perceive esthetically, he must remake his past experiences so that they can enter integrally into a new pattern" (p. 138). And it is the execution and production of this new pattern, one more determined by his perception of the form required to construct a consummating experience that is faithful to the subject matter, rather than one that is mechanically decided upon in advance by the application of some prepressed form, that will provide the work with its function of refreshing our perceptions and attitudes toward the facts and contingencies of experience.

Needless to say, the relationship between the creation of consummatory, aesthetic experience and the project of self-realization is dynamic and ongoing, as it must be under Dewey's conception of life-as-process. We need to recall this to mind to rebut the argument that if all experiences were consummatory in the manner indicated here, then life itself would be unutterably boring. Dewey's general account of experience commits him to the position that the achievement of self-realization can only be had to the extent that we remain aware that we can never reach a point of stasis, some existential nirvana in which all desire and striving ceases. Rather, life is a process of becoming, one in which the existence of frustrations and problems make the existence of consummatory experience possible. Our feelings of satisfaction from our earthly pilgrimage may lie more in the journey, with its pauses for self-doubt and examination, than in our arrival at any celestial city of complete and total self-knowledge.

CONCLUSION

Throughout this chapter, we have taken pains at various moments to reiterate the fact that for Dewey experience is an interaction of organism and environment that has both spatial and temporal dimensions. It is crucial to note here that as late as 1949 in *Knowing and the Known*, on which Dewey collaborated with Arthur F. Bentley, the idea of an organic *interaction* had been altered to the idea of a *transaction*. This important shift in terminology signaled that under this more rigorous conception of the organic, both components in the event are subject to change, to alteration. Not only do the components mutually condition each other in the process, but they themselves are altered, in however small a way. Temporal seriality, then, while it may for Dewey (1960b) be the "very essence" (p. 229) of the human individual, most assuredly does not imply that life is merely "one damn thing after another." To adopt this view would be to take a very lopsided perspective on causality, particularly in a post-Freudian world where we are accustomed to methods that purport to be able to root out the hidden wellsprings of motivation and neurosis. What is clear, however, is that it is not simply a feature of the biographical project alone to bring to light and place in conjunction for us the subtly formative incidents in an individual's life-in-time, but that the autobiographical project is also concerned with reconstructing and bringing into focus the nature of the transactions that have been instrumental in making us who we are. And yet, if our discussion of Dewey's notion of a consummatory experience signifies anything, it is that even as we attempt to reconstruct our past experiences, to provide them with a retrospective pattern they may not have held for us at the initial moment of the experience, *we are also constructing ourselves*, creating a fictional representation, an art object whose first audience and interpreter is ourselves, and from which process we may be able to extract some idea of the truth of our existence. Thus, clearly implicated in any autobiographical urge, and as an integral part of what I have been calling the aesthetics of self-realization, is a concept of self-the-artist, a concept that does not supersede self-the-scientist, but one in which the latter is subsumed and brought to fulfillment. By embarking on the unending journey of self-realization, through whatever medium (words, paint, music), individuals can indeed become the authors of their own life stories and in charge of the way they wish to represent themselves to the world.

Generally speaking, much of our exposition and discussion in this chapter has taken place on a level of abstraction consistent with the argument that would see in Dewey's work a source of educational warrants for autobiography as well as the framework that forms that conceptual bridge required to move literary theory over into educational territory. In educational terms, then, we can begin to see how the notions of history and fiction, which we discovered in the preceding chapter and which contained one of the major tensions to be found within any theory of autobiography, are rediscovered here completely implicated in the aesthetic agenda that is the culmination and ideal end of arguably the most fully developed theory of education currently at our disposal. Thus within Dewey's (and Mead's) account of the socially constructed nature of the self and mind, within his principles of inquiry or reflective thinking, and in his idea of consummatory experience that leads to what I have been calling an aesthetics of self-realization, can be found translated into educational language those features that in effect define the province of autobiography itself.

Clearly much else of importance for the place of autobiography in education is implicit in this exposition and interpretation of Dewey's work. What has been particularly in evidence, however, is the realization that we can maintain with an increasing sense of confidence our belief that contemporary reliance on autobiography and autobiographical acts is a logical extension of the movement begun decades ago by progressive educators and that is being refashioned today, for example in the whole language movement within language arts, as well as by teacher-educators as a way of reclaiming the nature of their students' educational experiences (Abbs, 1976; Grumet, 1981). Consequently, the practical task of situating autobiography in the curriculum, especially within language arts where there exists ample opportunity to foster the construction of the self in writing, will be our concern in the next chapter. There we will begin to observe that in the real world of the classroom, the philosophical and theoretical ideals expounded in this and the preceding chapter are indeed brought to earth as the autobiographical urge comes in contact with the politics of self-knowledge.

4   Autobiography and English Language Education

I suggest that the area in which language operates in English lessons is that of personal experience, in other words, relations with other people, the identity of the individual—the relations between the ego and the environment.

James Britton, 1970b

This chapter seeks to account for the status and role of autobiography in the domain of theory and practice in English teaching. I will be concerned initially with exploring how it has been articulated within the work of specific theorists in the United Kingdom. In particular, the ideas of James Britton will occupy our attention, since a strong argument could be made that his thinking has exerted a preeminent influence on the manner in which much language arts teaching now proceeds worldwide. One probable reason for the attraction many teachers in the United Kingdom and elsewhere have discovered in Britton's ideas is their democratic promise, a promise that stands in sharp contrast to a language arts curriculum otherwise dominated by a differential system of examinations that reflects versions of English deemed appropriate for pupils of varying social classes and abilities (Gorman, 1988; Lawton & Chitty, 1988). I will demonstrate later, how-ever, that a significant irony lies at the heart of this attraction, and that to analyze the role autobiography occupies in Britton's theory of lan-guage and learning will serve to highlight more specifically the partic-ular nature of that attraction. In addition, my analysis will also offer points of focus for one of this chapter's primary descriptive purposes: namely, to uncover the contexts and concepts required to ascertain how autobiography has found its way into the language arts curriculum and how it stands in relation to some of the more publicly professed aims of the discipline.

I propose to follow an organizational scheme that will allow me to inspect and comment on several key areas. First, although a number of commentators (Allen, 1980; Ball, 1987; Barnes, Barnes, & Clarke, 1984; Light, 1983) have taken to calling the practices within English teaching inspired by Britton's work a kind of "new orthodoxy," this designation is too simplistic and suggests that Britton's ideas have all but swept away any resistance. On the contrary, as I attempt to situate autobiography within the politics of the profession, conflict, dissent, and debate have rarely been livelier. Interestingly enough, although the two major opponents in the British end of this debate (the so-called "Cambridge" and "London" schools) part company on the stress placed by each on their separate visions of a literature-centered (Cambridge) versus a language-centered (London) curriculum for English, both are agreed on a child-centered notion of education. This focus has led to a common concentration on the child's experience and the child's place within the cultural formations of school and society. As we will discover, whether as a rallying cry or as a deliberately theorized position, autobiography as one way of reflecting on both self and experience begins to assume a crucial role in these conceptions of language arts teaching. I will, of course, flesh out the terms of these conceptions, and tease out their implications for a view of autobiography in the language arts curriculum.

Second, in a longer section, our attention will be given over entirely to the work of James Britton. In a series of short subsections I want to inspect briefly the ideas of two theorists who have exerted a lasting influence on Britton's own thinking, namely, D. W. Harding and George Kelly. I will argue that although Britton's theory gained significantly in terms of its economy by reducing Harding's four perceptual "stances" to two (the participant and spectator roles), Britton perhaps overstates his claim that spectator-role discourse alone can provide a student with a way of building that world representation he finds articulated in Kelly's theory of personal constructs. Taken under this proviso, then, I will stress the singular features of Harding's and Kelly's positions that enable Britton to utilize the psychological insights of both theorists. As well, some attention will be given to the work of H. G. Widdowson, since in recent additions to his theory Britton has used certain of Widdowson's ideas to further warrant and elaborate on his own position. I will undertake to show that the view of language and learning espoused by Britton and warranted by the work of these thinkers is supplemented throughout by a strong concern for autobiography, an impulse whose clearest expression is contained in the logic of Britton's notion of the spectator role, a term that will occupy us more fully later.

With this in place, a further section will address not only to what extent Britton's ideas have begun to shape and inform the practice of English teaching in the United Kingdom, Canada, the United States, Australia, and elsewhere, but more particularly will address how provision is made in the United Kingdom for the writing of autobiographical discourses within language arts curricula largely driven by the existence of external state-run examinations. To this end, close attention will be given to Barnes, Barnes, and Clarke's (1984) important longitudinal study, published as *Versions of English*. The reader can anticipate a discussion and critique that will range freely from contexts and concepts developed in the earlier part of this chapter outward toward a more comprehensive view of autobiography in the curriculum. This concluding discussion, by building on Britton's work, offers a theoretically more coherent account of the genre, as well as recommending its use in an expanded role for the teacher of English. Specifically, if we come to conceive of autobiography as essentially fictional in character, and combine this insight with the empirically validated finding whereby the construction of narratives is the method of dealing with "the personal" preferred by a majority of students, then we can begin to envision English language arts classrooms as sites governed by a potentially more meaningful set of discursive and instructional practices.

The overall import of the chapter, then, is not only the extent to which it describes the contours of an influential paradigm within English language education, but as it makes a stronger case for an enlarged conception of autobiography as a master discourse within the language arts curriculum. By uncovering within autobiography a significant range of political, social, and educational concerns that have a direct bearing on the way different groups of children are enabled or constrained from reflecting on their experiences, we may be able to distinguish more clearly the kind of role discourse itself can play in constructing particular kinds of human subjectivity.

AUTOBIOGRAPHY AND THE POLITICS OF ENGLISH TEACHING

In a lively and useful article entitled "London Looks at English Theory: Hurry Up Please, It's Time!" Maguire and Washington (1983), a Canadian and an American, recount the highlights of their experiences of a six-week course at the London Institute of Education. Interestingly, a major part of their article is devoted to outlining the cardinal features of the two schools of thought that have been vying for ascendancy within English education for about twenty years. Perhaps owing to the site of their coursework, Maguire and Washington (1983) call the theory emanating from the London Institute the "orthodoxy school" (p. 26), and associate it with figures such as Britton, Dixon, Stratta, and Wilkinson, while the other school, called "their opponents" (p. 26) and centered in Cambridge, is associated with figures such as Abbs, Whitehead, Holbrook, and Thompson. That in 1983 these commentators could find how the theoretical strings of English language education were still vibrating from their initial plucking in the mid- to late 1960s attests, among other things, to the strength and persistence of the issues that divide the field itself. There have been many attempts to delineate the precise nature of those disagreements, attempts that have a direct bearing on our present inquiry into the status of autobiography within English education. What follows is a brief excursion into the ideas of these opposing camps insofar as we can extract from them examples that will serve to elucidate our present concerns.

There is not space here to deal extensively with the emergence of English as a distinct discipline, nor with many of the claims made on its behalf as a key subject within the school curriculum. Suffice it to say for now that Allen's (1980) attempt to locate that chimerical center within English teaching, that vision of unity within the subject in which "the various modes of language (reading, writing, speaking, listening) interact with each other in the development of competence" (p. 11), achieved at best a minor, and qualified, success. The notion of a center, he concluded, was without question ambiguous, and, as he states, fails "to describe in any firm way the *relationship* between literature and the rest of the subject" (Allen, 1980, p. 11, emphasis in original). Allen is able to trace, as did Mathieson (1975) before him and more recently Doyle (1989), a direct line back to Matthew Arnold's ideas in the nineteenth century, ideas that for the Cambridge school made literature the strongest candidate in any notion of a center. Contemporary expression of this Arnoldian view Allen finds articulated in the ideas of Denys Thompson, a disciple of F. R. Leavis's and longtime editor of *Use of English*. According to Thompson (1973), literature, dealing as it does with the expression of experience, is ideally the medium whereby several key educational outcomes can be promoted, if not assured. Literature sensitizes us to the myriad uses of language and hence can facilitate communication; literature fosters tolerance, humanity, and understanding, those consummate human values that have been misplaced in an epoch of mass advertising and a general decline in values; and literature makes for growth: In a hostile world where personal and moral growth is damaged, literature offers a restorative, a healing alternative.

By "literature" Thompson did not necessarily mean "great literature," although in practice the kind of refining of the sensibilities implied by his thinking might best be found in studying the monuments of the English literary heritage. Although a like-minded figure like Frank Whitehead found Thompson's emphasis on the uses of literature problematic in that literature could be "used" to promote anything from a political message to the focus for a linguistic exercise, Whitehead himself (1966) asserted that "what needs to be assessed after all is not knowledge about literature, but the power to read it and respond to it" (p. 18). Just how the child was to read and respond to literature was less clear, but it boiled down in large measure to a variant of New Critical respect for close reading and "the words on the page."

Regardless of these criticisms of Thompson, Whitehead agreed that with literature at the center, the teacher of English could indeed find a mission worthy of the highest calling. With their Manichean view of culture and society wherein the forces of evil, symbolized by the mass media in all its forms, could only be overthrown by doses of great literature liberally administered, the imperatives of the Cambridge school were based on the promulgation of an elite view of knowledge. On the other hand, the London school challenged this view by stressing the centrality of language of school students, both spoken and written.

Stephen Ball's (1988) inquiry into the politics of English teaching in the years 1970 through 1985 states that the celebration by the London school of the immediate life, culture, and language of the student meant, in effect, a celebration of "the culture and language of the working class. Below the level of opposed knowledge bases there are also opposed ideologies and political commitments" (p. 21). A large part of the challenge to traditional pedagogies and authority consisted of an attempt to subordinate the role of literature and to privilege instead the pupils' own experience, talk, and writing. Therefore the ideological import of the London school's insistence on the child's own language carries with it strong political overtones. According to the London school's way of thinking, in a class-ridden culture, working-class experience has been perennially silenced; in order to assist in breaking that silence, it behooves teachers to provide pupils with opportunities to talk and write about themselves in a personal way. In this way the writing of an autobiography makes the personal political; English can no longer be conceived wholly in Abbs's (1977) terms as "the celebration of the self through the art of symbolization" (p. 56). Rather, English teaching must now promote the self *as* symbol: Language is completely implicated in the construction of that self.

In addition to this, however, the literary critical approach made explicit in the views of the Cambridge school was to be eschewed at all costs; likewise the "cultural heritage" approach was to give way to more talk and drama, that is, to more oral than textual opportunities. As John Dixon put it in his influential book *Growth Through English* (1967), "A sense of the social system of writing has so inhibited and overawed many teachers that they have never given a pupil the feeling that what he writes is his own" (p. 44). This sense of ownership, of having a stake in the active creation of knowledge in the cut-and-thrust of the classroom, had enormous implications for the method and manner of purveying English in the schools. It meant a movement away from traditional notions of a teacher-centered classroom, with its attendant epistemology whereby the teacher filled up the empty vessels that were the pupils' minds, to a more cooperative mode that stressed group work, project work, and individual, high-interest assignments with an epistemology based on the active, personal appropriation of meaning. So it is that two areas of greatest concern for the student of autobiography can be discovered in the schools' views of experience and of personal development. Let us consider first the contentious and awkward world of experience.

In the view of the Cambridge school, experience is in Allen's (1980) words "from one viewpoint wholly private and *personal*, concerned with self-expression for one's own private purposes" (p. 10). However, experiences may also be seen as cultural, in that we experience what we do "as a result of our upbringing in a particular time and place through a particular mediating form of language and perception" (p. 10). The work of Thompson and others presupposes a relationship between personal and cultural experiences through the medium of literature, presumably on the assumption that literature is a form of ordered experience that allows us to reflect on our own experience at the same time as it provides an experience *in* the reading event itself. On the other hand, from the viewpoint of the London school, Maguire and Washington (1983) approve of Geoffrey Summerfield's attempt to locate a student's self "in the classroom galaxy with the world, the text, and the teacher" (p. 25) as part of a social process that is continuously in flux. They find Summerfield useful in suggesting how that world of private and public experiences outside the classroom is transformed in the world of the classroom, where personalities and texts interact within an institutional setting to provide a forum for coming to terms with "the personal." Self-expression here is catered for by finding ways to make public the private explorations of the experiencing child.

The London school's view of experience is claimed to be compatible in many respects with the epistemology of pragmatism that stresses the active and experiential nature of knowledge creation. It offers students a way of looking at life beyond their own experience through the agency of texts, a point that both schools would agree to; likewise, by bringing the students' own experiences into the classroom it does not sever contact with the real world outside the classroom walls, and hence validates a student's own experience as equally worthy of attention and respect.

In practice, however, this laudable aim was treated in different ways by the two schools. For Holbrook (1961), opportunities in reading and writing led to a psychiatric role for English wherein the products of student creativity exemplified in imaginative writing could be examined by the teacher/therapist for key moments in which the inner, private world of the child's psyche burst forth in the full flower of its Freudian symbolism. Consistent with his Freudian orientation, Holbrook believes that we pay the price of repression for the varied, and sometimes dubious, fruits of civilization. Creative writing releases in resymbolized form many of the students' repressed feelings. But this is not just a convenient way of blowing off psychic steam (although, surely, this is implied in any Freudian talking or writing cure); rather, it is to be concerned with how the forces in society become inscribed in the students' minds and bodies. How, in effect, has the student's self been constructed, and how can the student gain insight into that dynamic process to the extent of coming to terms with it, or better, of making the kinds of choices necessary to begin altering it? A tall order indeed for any psychiatrist, let alone for any ordinary teacher or writing program.

On the other hand, John Dixon, in *Growth Through English* (1967), adopted Piagetian frames of reference that he stressed in one of his models of English teaching, namely, the focus on cognitive growth. This model allowed for a total concentration on the child-as-center; here, the primacy of the child's experience and an emphasis on a developmental psychology of learning merge in a conception of the child that was to exert an increasing influence on the practice of English teaching. If concern for the child's maturity or growth is the *telos* of English teaching, and if one's point of departure is, like the London school's, the pupil's language, then language and experience are seen to interact so that the modes of expression available to the pupil influence the nature of the experience from the beginning. Here, literature, for example, is simply another voice in the classroom, one that adds to the store of experience, but not necessarily a finer or better voice. For someone like Dixon, language has many purposes: It can give shape to experience, it can build theories about the world, it can celebrate important moments. Hence the "passive" use of language (reading and listening) was to be replaced by more "active" elements (talking and writing). This new rhetoric was required in order for students to reflect on, as well as to build, their own representational worlds.

From the foregoing it ought to be clear that it is a very short step from a commitment to a child-centered view that emphasizes how language is used for a variety of purposes to a conception of English in which Gray's (1982) loose constructionist view of our culture's fascination with self is not only encouraged but mandatory. For as Maguire and Washington (1983) learned from their course as part of the London school's catechism, "All children are fluent in autobiographical story telling" (p. 25). Autobiography, as arguably one of the most important forms of discourse inherited from the Romantics, seems tailor-made for a theory that places such store on reclaiming the child's own voice and experience.

And yet what remains to be considered is the relationship between autobiography as what Light (1983) calls a form of "narcissistic withdrawal" (p. 72) and the more socially (and socialistically) oriented imperatives of collaboration and community. The kind of English practice that encourages explorations in autobiography as a gesture toward the achievement of a greater self-consciousness can remain doomed to futility if it simply operates in a vacuum, unconnected to any larger vision of social transformation. If the move toward autobiographical modes of writing is a consequence of a Romantic inheritance that celebrates the growth of the child, and also a particular view of the self as free, neither unfixed by hereditary social position nor valorized by particular social and economic institutions, then it must be rescued from its tendency to stop short at the moment when it could be pressed harder into greater social service. Indeed, Britton (1982) himself, like Dewey before him, has several times voiced the observation that the process of individuation conceals a central paradox; namely, that "going one's way, fulfilling one's own particular blueprint" (p. 160) is only, if at all, reconciled socially "in a society that corporately we have constructed" (p. 160).

Although we must now leave the schools of thought and the politics of English teaching in temporary abeyance, enough has been said for the moment to indicate that autobiography stands in intimate relation to the plethora of ideas put forward in an effort to rethink the nature of the discipline. We turn instead to the work of one man, James Britton, since any search for the role of the personal in language education must take account of his singular contribution. Once again autobiography will emerge as a forceful melody in the chorus that Britton has taught us to sing.

JAMES BRITTON:
LEARNING TO USE THE LANGUAGE OF THE SELF

I want to begin by attending briefly to an instance in which Britton takes up the relationship among teaching, language, and learning. This instance is not totally arbitrary, but has been selected to represent the kind of thinking for which Britton has made himself known. What I want to accomplish in advance of inquiring more precisely into specific influences on Britton's theory and their importance for our developing notions of autobiography is to provide a sample of Britton's thinking, one that will demonstrate how intuitively appealing Britton has been for language arts teachers.

In "Their Language and Our Teaching," an address given at the 1970 N.A.T.E. (National Association of Teachers of English) conference, Britton set out to rethink what happens when a successful teaching-learning event takes place. The target of his attack here is the pedagogy of the teacher-centered classroom, or what Britton (1970b) calls (after John Newsom) the "jug and mug technique" (p. 6). This is analogous to the empty vessel theory of learning we encountered in the second section of this chapter: The child is the mug and the teacher is the jug. To learn means that the teacher tips the contents of his mind into the waiting container. Britton wants to claim, of course, that under this scenario the contribution of the learner has been vastly underestimated. But more than this, Britton wishes to take a further step and claim that "it is a common error to *over*estimate the difference between *being told* and *finding out for yourself*" (p. 7, emphasis in original). By drawing on the work of the Russian learning theorist Vygotsky and the American psychologist Carl Rogers, Britton moves the locus of his discussion to a notion of self-discovered learning in which "truth [can be] personally appropriated and assimilated in experience" (p. 7). To succeed in this task learners must have at their disposal the means to move from what is already known to something new. Although Vygotsky's zone of proximal development is never specifically named, it is clear that the role Britton envisages for the teacher is the advisory one of assisting in stimulating the pupil who is being told to find something out to actually accomplish this task. From the pupil's point of view this means trying "to create a personal context for whatever it is he is being told" (p. 9). At the root of Britton's ideas on how best to bring about this end is the key notion of expressive speech. Expressive speech is "talk that is close to the *self* of the speaker" (p. 9, emphasis in original); it is inherently social as well. The outcome of recognizing its importance is that by talking, students begin to learn from each other. Learning from each other and learning with each other are therefore inextricably woven together.

This view undercuts a notion that considers learning as mere acquisition of inert knowledge; rather, it involves, in Britton's words, "a process of making finer and finer distinctions, and so building a more and more complex picture of the world" (p. 12). In Britton's economy of giving and taking, talk is the currency; however, it requires an initial investment of commitment on the part of the child before he or she can reap the dividend of that complex picture of self and society.

This instance was chosen to highlight features of Britton's thinking that emerge from virtually any random selection of his writing. Although we will go on to examine in more detail the theoretical bases that lie behind his assertions and warrant his particular emphases, I want to focus for a moment on some of their more immediate and obvious implications. First of all, a classroom (and here Britton has the elementary classroom in mind) is theorized as a site where, through the medium of expressive speech, the student's experience can serve as the raw material in a meaning-making process that works to resymbolize reality. But more than this: If students further resymbolize their experience in writing, another option is opened up; they can operate on that representation as an artlike production. In this way the child's own writing—what John Dixon calls the literature of the classroom—becomes the key texts to which everyone pays attention. It is conceivable, then, that at least one logical consequence for the English classroom is that books themselves might become redundant and that an entire curriculum could be manufactured (literally) from the pupils' own writing.

This instance serves to demonstrate on several levels the ramifications for pedagogy that Britton's views of the child and language and learning promote. What I now want to examine is the genesis of some of the major elements in Britton's thinking. Britton's theory is boldly eclectic; he synthesizes ideas and concepts from figures working in a variety of disciplines: philosophy, cognitive psychology, linguistics. I will deal in turn with the main ideas of D. W. Harding, George Kelly, and H. G. Widdowson as they find themselves incorporated in Britton's theory.

D. W. Harding

In his essay "Spectator Role and the Beginnings of Writing" (1982a), Britton recounts an anecdote concerning himself and D. W. Harding. In 1968, Britton had prepared an advance paper entitled "Response to Literature" for discussion at the Anglo-American seminar at Dartmouth. In that paper he proposed what he called an "unorthodox" view of literature, which had found a first crude articulation as early as 1963 in a book entitled *The Arts and Current Tendencies in Education.* Basically, Britton maintained a distinction between the roles of participant and spectator. In his early (1963) formulation he differentiated between them this way:

> If I describe what has happened to me in order to get my hearer to do something for me . . . then I remain a participant in my own affairs and invite him to become one. If, on the other hand, I merely want to interest him, so that he savors with me the joys and sorrows and surprises of my past experience and appreciates with me the intricate pattern of events, then not only do I invite him to be a spectator, but I myself am a spectator of my own experience. (p. 39)

Literature was, for Britton, "language in the role of the spectator and so related to the spoken form, gossip about events" (Britton, 1982a, p. 49). The study group responsible for debating Britton's paper at the conference was under the chairmanship of D. W. Harding; after the meeting, Harding approached Britton and inquired if Britton was familar with his own papers putting forward a similar view. As a consequence, Britton (1982) read "for the first time" (p. 50), in Dartmouth College Library, Harding's "The Role of the Onlooker" (1937) and "Psychological Processes in the Reading of Fiction" (1962).

What Britton discovered in Harding's papers was a position that articulated the idea that we use language for two distinct purposes: to have an effect on our actual world and to test our ideas about that world without committing ourselves through action. In order to expand on that notion, Harding (1937) distinguished four modes of activity:

1. Actually doing things, what he calls "an operative response" (p. 247);
2. Intellectual comprehension, which "stops at comprehension and involves no attempt to control or modify what is comprehended" (p. 247);
3. Looking and listening to things "for the sake of experiencing them and organizing them at the level of perception" (p. 247); and
4. Detached evaluation—"it is in this that the role of the spectator typically consists" (p. 248).

Harding (1937) devotes the greatest share of attention to explaining the significance of detached evaluation, since for him it possesses "the utmost importance in building up, confirming and modifying all but the very simplest of our values" (p. 252).

Harding provides a wealth of supporting detail about the kinds of social relationships that become possible when we adopt the detached, evaluative role of the spectator. More important for the points he wants to make about literature, however, is the range of possibilities opened up "when we pass from direct experience of our surroundings to that represented symbolically" (p. 255). Harding was aware that symbolic representation is commonly thought of as a way by which one person communicates with another. However, he wants to claim that much of our representation of experience "may be entirely private, as in daydreaming and solitary make-believe play" (p. 255). Here we represent possibilities *and* evaluate them at the same time. But when we stop representing experience privately and begin to communicate, two important features arise. One is cooperative make-believe play, and the other is gossip. For Harding, the playwright and the novelist all do basically the same thing as the gossip: raise an interesting situation and expect listeners (readers) to agree that it is so. In literature, then, the author "invites his audience to share in an exploration . . . of his and their common interests; and, as a corollary, to refine or modify their value judgements" (Harding, 1937, p. 258). Britton's (1982a) gloss on Harding's notion is interesting here. He considers it no distortion of Harding's ideas to suggest that "as participants we *apply* our value systems, but as spectators we *generate and refine* the system itself" (p. 51, emphasis in original). By adopting the role of spectator we are freed from the constraints of applying our value systems directly and instead can test and evaluate them. Works of fiction or drama as forms of narrative invite us to be onlookers "in the evaluation of some possibility of experience" (Harding, 1962, p. 138).

When Britton later directed these ideas to the development of writing, Harding's four stances or roles were reduced to two—participant and spectator—and were related to a continuum of language functions, namely, the transactional, the poetic, and the expressive. The transactional is used to get things done in the world; the poetic is used to produce an art form; and the expressive indicates to others the personality and personal world of the individual.

The problem with Britton's reduction of Harding's four roles to simply the participant-spectator continuum is that he has not indicated clearly enough that part of learning any other subject or discipline is precisely the ability to adopt a spectatorlike, critical role. Students in a wide range of subject area classes are being provided with such opportunities for similar reasons. For example, many science educators strive for moments that will provide both personal engagement and opportunities for reflection. However, in the case of English, Britton's notion of the spectator marks out an area of linguistic territory of its own that is given over to the construction of specifically art-like verbal objects. Still, we ought to keep in mind those similar, independently developed pedagogies and practices in other disciplines as we embark on a more detailed appreciation of Britton's work.

Britton himself has commented extensively on the relationship between the categories described above and their consequences for the development of writing abilities. What is of particular interest to us is how Britton has marked out and theorized the kind of territory autobiography might occupy in this scheme, given the emphasis on informal storytelling implied in both his and Harding's notion of literature as gossip. Britton (1981) believes that in the very process of perceiving the world "we give and find shape, pattern, order" (p. 7). Furthermore, in the way we tell the stories of our lives we give and find another shape. Britton wants to emphasize that we both "give" and "find" shape since shape, pattern, and order exist in the world "irrespective of our human perceiving and intepreting" (p. 7). What, however, are we to make of children's untutored attempts at narrating, and hence repossessing, the events of their own life stories? Britton (1981) asserts that "Gossip and the child's unshaped narrative, autobiographical or fictional, is 'art-like' but not art" (p. 6); that is, they are artlike performances that employ spectator-role discourse but lack the unity and coherence implicit in the achieved form of the work of art.

In addition, Britton has also provided us with an extended discussion of the place autobiography occupies for him within spectator-role discourse. He begins from the premise that writers who take up the spectator role are under no obligation to tell the truth: "What they write may be predominantly fictional or substantially true" (1983, p. 27). Since a great deal of autobiographical writing is written from the spectator's point of view and involves the kind of self-consciousness that makes self an object, it is indeed "a verbal construct" (p. 27). Britton distinguishes between a strictly "historical" use of autobiography "where the concern is not to recreate experience but to get the facts right" (p. 27) and a "literary" autobiography "where the writer tries to capture the quality of past experiences" (p. 27). According to this latter conception, "we might well be justified in dissociating 'the real me' of the author from 'the pretend me' of the narrator" (p. 27). Even if we grant that, if pressed, Britton could be more precise about what he feels a "real me" is, what the foregoing clearly points to is something we have encountered many times before: the distinction between autobiographical and fictional narrative is elusive and cannot be sustained with any degree of certainty.

In this connection Britton would have us recall the evaluative dimension within the spectator role. Whether we are gossiping or whether we are trying to shape an autobiography, we adopt in the attitudinal coloring of our discourse a particular evaluative stance. This coloration brings out "aspects of the original events which heighten the evaluation we are intent upon offering" (Britton, 1983, p. 27). In addition, says Britton (1983), these discursive embellishments or distortions "may well grow more marked the more we repeat the telling" (p. 27). To acknowledge as much is to take note of the extent to which autobiographical narrative is fictional in character and constructed to highlight those dimensions that adhere to any writing in the spectator role. Hence, from this position a clear conception of the child as artist begins to emerge. If the use of poetic language, that is, the language of literature, is employed not for doing something like giving orders but for making a verbal object (although, of course, to make is also to do), then the child engaged in giving shape to an autobiographical narrative is involved in exactly the same process as the novelist or dramatist. It follows, then, that a teacher of English who conceives of autobiography as simply the writing of personal history is failing to grasp Britton's essential point. By asking pupils to recount a simple chronology of dates and places and times, the storytelling potential within autobiography as a mode of artistic discourse is being greatly undervalued. Britton leaves entirely open the possibility for us to employ it in this way; in fact, to develop it as the form of narration that comes closest to giving a sense of order to our students' experiences is a task for English teaching that deserves greater attention than has been the case to this point.

As we have seen, Britton's indebtedness to Harding is focused on only one aspect within Harding's conception of the role of the onlooker. And yet that aspect—the importance of detached evaluation—has provided Britton with sufficient conceptual leverage to prise open a way to start making sense of the shifting position(s) of autobiography as a form of literary narrative. As a consequence of emphasizing this literary element, the Romantic notion of the child as artist has clearly emerged from the logic of pursuing this strand within Britton's theorizing of the role of the spectator. If we move now from Harding's contribution to Britton's thinking and take up the ideas of the psychologist George Kelly, we will be able to get a firmer hold on the *function* of autobiographical writing in a child-centered classroom given over to the evaluation of experience in narrative.

George Kelly

As we saw in the early part of the chapter, which dealt with the relative positions of the two competing schools of thought in English teaching, both groups rested key elements of their theories on particular views of the nature of experience in relation to language. For those influenced by Britton, to witness the movement from oral to written forms of discourse in the child is to follow the evolution of what Britton (1983) calls "the story world" (p. 3). Drawing on the work of Applebee (1980) and others on children's narrative writing, Britton reiterates one of Applebee's major points; namely, that story writing provides for the child "a release from the demands of immediate response" (p. 9). When the child is so released, a progressive sense of pleasure can develop from both the child's active preoccupation with the power of the written language and from the complexities of the relationship between his story world and the "real" world of the child's own experiences.

Britton (1983) wants to deny the existence of a dichotomy between a "real" and a "pretend" world for reasons he finds in the work of Cassirer (1944), Langer (1960), and Sapir (1961) between our status as a symbol-using animal and the way in which we represent the world to ourselves from the crucible of our experience and from our successive encounters with it. Although there is some suggestion that the real and pretend worlds cannot be distinguished, rather than being equally valued, writing in the spectator role is a method Britton (1983) offers as an alternative and appealing type of behavior, one in which *"we may operate directly upon our world picture without seeking outcomes in actuality"* (p. 25, emphasis in original). This kind of behavior, whereby we can improvise on our world picture with no intention to act, is for Britton (1983) analogous to other such forms of activity as daydreaming, where we can invent "flattering visions of the future . . . sweeten our disappointments or recover our self-composure" (p. 25). These activities serve to preserve the unity and coherence in the world picture or world representation by which we live.

Britton finds this view of the relationship between language and experience consistent and compatible with the theory of personal constructs, or "constructive alternativism" (Kelly, 1963, p. 3), proposed by the American psychologist George Kelly. At the center of Kelly's (1963) personal construct theory lies the abstraction he calls "man-the-scientist" [sic] (p. 4), a figure that emerged for us in the previous chapter from the work of John Dewey. Like Dewey, Kelly wants to consider this collocation an "abstraction of all mankind and not a concrete classification of a particular man" (p. 4). In his guise as man-the-scientist, Kelly believes with Dewey that our ultimate aim is "to predict and control" (p. 5). In this sense, then, human behavior is experimental: Like the scientist, we draw from past experience certain hypotheses that pertain to any present encounter and go about testing and reforming them in the light of what actually happens. In this way we constantly refine the predictive bases of our behavior and hence begin to assume an increasing measure of control over the nature of our choices and the shape and direction of our lives. For Britton, however, there are two distinct aspects of this construct system, aspects which, as will become apparent, speak directly and relevantly to the multifaceted concept of autobiography. First of all, there is what Britton (1981) calls a " 'knowledge' aspect—an organization of the inferences from experience as to what that world is like" (p. 6). This knowledge undergoes a constant process of amendment and change based on our experience of the world and our reactions to it. Second, there is a " 'value' aspect—an organization of how much and in what ways we *care*" (p. 6). From this aspect we can chart the manifold ways in which our sympathies, feelings, and emotions are engaged or disengaged. From the knowledge aspect what we require is "a rational, logical, consistent set of constructs" (Britton, 1981, p. 6), one that, like any good and elegant theory, will assist us in extending and refining the predictive elements in our system. The value aspect, however, requires a different mode, "one that in its perfected form we call 'art'" (p. 6); and as we have seen from our earlier discussion of the spectator role, what art or artlike performances offer is the possibility of a progressive experience of order, that unity and coherence which underlies our daily lives but a sense of which we may have lost.

We can now, I think, begin to understand how provocative this constructivist alternative really is. Autobiography can be functionally conceived as a mode of written discourse in which the more it approaches the condition of art, the more it is capable of disclosing the paths by which our representations of self and world have come to be formed. And yet this view of autobiography as a form of literary discourse involves a change, to use Britton's terms, from viewing its function as essentially expressive to predominantly poetic, and brings with it a number of problems that attend all forms of artlike discourse that aspire to the condition of a complex verbal symbol. Britton is aware that any theory that promotes autobiography as a way of discovering, testing, and reforming the nature of our world representations must attempt to deal with the thorny problem of the first-person narrator, the "I" who recounts and shapes his or her presentation of experience. To assist him in this task, Britton (1982) enlists the help of the stylistician H. G. Widdowson, and it is to Widdowson's work that we now turn.

H. G. Widdowson

In the chapter "The Nature of Literary Communication" in his book *Stylistics and the Teaching of Literature* (1975), Widdowson's basic task is to explain the difference between the literary and nonliterary use of identifying pronouns so as to gain an appreciation for the special characteristics of "the literary message" (p. 51). First, in such forms of nonliterary discourses as diaries and letters "there is no distinction between sender and addresser and the writer is assumed to be 'telling the truth,' describing real events, expressing his own feelings" (p. 53). In other words, the writer of the letter or diary can be held responsible for the feelings and opinions so expressed. In Widdowson's admittedly arguable example, love letters count as evidence in a court of law, but love poems do not. Second, in many forms of written discourse the sender/addresser communicates from a particular role: businessman, lawyer, professor. What the sender says is largely determined by this role, "and he is not at liberty to express his own individual sentiments at will" (Widdowson, 1975, p. 52). To obtrude private or idiosyncratic thoughts into such communications would be to breach the nature of the public roles individuals assume by virtue of a certain position in society. Widdowson concludes, "We may say that the 'I' of conventional communication refers to the social persona and not to the individual person" (p. 52). Last, in literary writing, however, the "I" *does* refer to the "thoughts, impressions, imaginings and perceptions of the individual person" (pp. 52–53). But it is not the writer as the sender of the message that the "I" refers to; rather, it is "the inner self that the writer is objectifying" (p. 53), and this act of objectification "involves detaching the self and observing it as if it were a third person identity" (p. 53). Hence, we can*not* assume that the sender and addresser of the literary message are the same, since the experiences described in the literary message may well be ones that the writer imagines himself undergoing. It is this aspect of artistic convention that relieves the writer from "any social responsibility for what he says in the first person" (p. 53). Although it is clear that writers of literature often have a social purpose, the success of a particular novel is unlikely to be measured in terms of any action it might provoke. The writer, *qua* writer, expresses a certain personal vision or view of reality in the hope that the reader, "as an *observer* of reality, might then feel constrained to act in a certain way" (p. 53, emphasis in original).

It is here perhaps that Widdowson's notion of the objectification of the inner self accords well with Harding's concept of the function of detached evaluation within the spectator role. Likewise, the hypothesis-testing and reforming of our world pictures suggested in Kelly's theory of personal constructs seems to provide the kind of warrant Britton requires in order to maintain his commitment to a child-centered view of education and the intimate connection between language and learning. In addition, the knowledge and value aspects implicit in Kelly's theory also support a notion of the heuristic potential within the literary use of autobiography. The activity of shaping required by the use of narrative as a way of giving pattern and order to the child's experience contains both cognitive and affective elements. From the relative safety of the autobiographer's persona, the child can be freed from the restrictions that adhere to other uses of first-person discourse; consequently, the admixture of reality and fantasy that goes into the makeup of the child's world picture can be brought under the patterning of experience associated with all art-like performances.

Summary

This brief inquiry into the source of the warrants for Britton's theory of language and learning was undertaken in order to abstract from his views focal points that might prove immediately relevant to our specific interest in autobiography. What has begun to emerge, both explicitly and implicitly, from Britton's work is a conception of autobiography of some complexity. Autobiography approaches the condition of art the more it follows the shaping and patterning procedures applicable to the achieved form of a literary production. Unlike Dewey in education and many commentators on autobiography in literary theory, if Britton stops short at saying, or declines to embrace the full consequences of saying, that the child's self is constructed within autobiographical narrative, his appeals to the work of Kelly and Widdowson provide ample proof of his assertions that narrative in general, and autobiography in particular, is an exemplary method whereby the child can come to grips with the wide range of experiences that impinge upon his sense of identity.

Britton (1983), as was Dewey, is fond of repeating a distinction he found in the work of William James wherein James likens human consciousness to the difference between "flights" and "perches" in the behavior of birds. Our perches—those contemplative intermissions where we use language to reconstruct past experiences or to imagine alternative ways of construing them—might be a useful way to conceive of one possible function for autobiography. To invite the child to take part in an odyssey of self-discovery where the thousand faces of the hero/heroine can be sketched, touched up, and reworked in that endlessly fascinating project of tinkering with the self is to recognize Narcissus rather than Antaeus as the ruling mythological figure. Britton himself has only partially and unsatisfactorily gestured toward addressing the educational issue of how to provide for the transfer from this narcissistic withdrawal to the theater of social engagement and responsibility. It would appear on the face of it, however, that the child's artlike performances require little justification, or that their utility as means to the creation of an identity are too obvious to require extensive comment. It is precisely here, in the translation from theory into practice, that the acid test of Britton's views can perhaps be found. Of course it is arguable whether Britton can be held responsible for the manner in which his suggestions have found a home in the schools; but since his influence has been considerable, we might anticipate an echo of his thinking, however far away and attenuated, in the daily practice of English teaching. As was indicated earlier,

Douglas and Dorothy Barnes (Barnes et al., 1984) completed a three-year longitudinal study on the versions of English as a school subject purveyed in several schools in the north of England. The scope and rigor of this study make it a suitable point of departure from the ideal world of theory into the contingent and unalterably messy world of practice.

AUTOBIOGRAPHY IN THE ENGLISH CLASSROOM

It would overburden the particular objectives of this chapter as a whole to embark on a detailed commentary of the Barneses' lengthy and farreaching research project. Indeed, this section of the chapter itself will suffer the inevitable fate of all those who commit "the heresy of paraphrase" (Brooks, 1947, p. 192). And yet insofar as is possible, I will attempt to provide sufficient detail and explanation in order to serve the main object of our inquiry: the present status of autobiography within the English curriculum. It may be worth bearing in mind, however, that *Versions of English* is set entirely within the context of the institutional practices of schools in the United Kingdom, with their attendant and often bewildering array of school-leaving certificates. However, I believe that classroom practice is similar enough in most parts of the world to warrant investing our time and attention in the Barneses' research.

The material upon which the Barneses' claims are based is, as ethnographers would have it, "thick description"; it is immensely rich and varied in its content. Included are lesson observations, field notes, tape recordings, and interviews and informal discussions with teachers and pupils, as well as over 770 items of student writing. The Barneses' interest in this material was not principally to discover how writing was being taught, but to determine how criteria are transmitted that enable pupils to make the appropriate choices of content and approach to the writing event—choices on which they will ultimately be judged by external examiners. These criteria of assessment the Barneses see as falling into two groups: surface and deep criteria. Surface criteria such as spelling, punctuation, conventions of layout, and genre are, he claims, relatively easy to communicate (although that does not guarantee that they will always be applied correctly); deep criteria are much harder to pin down but have a great influence on grading procedures.

Examples of deep criteria might include such items as emphasis, style, tone, and atmosphere. For the Barneses (Barnes et al., 1984), these deep criteria are of paramount interest because they not only amount to "a set of preferred pictures of the world" (p. 70), but are in fact potentially "the deep criteria for living" (p. 70). The other important point is that these deep criteria are more available to some pupils than to others owing to a range of cultural advantages in the home, thus ensuring success for some and difficulties, if not failure, for others. The Barneses believe that this cultural capital brought from the home exists in the form of "sensitivities and preferences for what amount to little more than differences of style and perspective" (p. 70). How pupils gain access to these deep criteria and how the English curriculum is differentially purveyed to those thought to possess or be deficient in these criteria is a key item on their agenda. By observing how pupils are prepared for writing, and by noting how teachers justify judgments regarding the kind of writing deemed appropriate for each group, the Barneses claim we will be in a stronger position to understand some distinct vagaries within the English curriculum. But since our focus is on autobiography as a form of private/personal writing, we will now turn to the Barneses' discussion of that mode in order to indicate some of the practical dilemmas students find themselves in when confronted by a request to write "personally."

Several salient points emerge from the Barneses' discussion of representative selections from hundreds of samples of writing. In many examples, what defined the piece as personal was not merely a topic that directed the pupil's attention toward private experience, "but the author's reflective reinterpretation of experience" (Barnes et al., 1984, p. 100). The writing event was used as an opportunity "to reconsider and reshape personal history" (p. 100); a common way for English teachers to express the same idea was to have the pupils "come to terms with their experiences." Another characteristic commonly found in the writing and valued by teachers was the adequate provision of realistic detail, a feature that seemed to guarantee "the author's implicit claim to a meticulous truthfulness to the texture of experience" (p. 100). Though this kind of detail is a common enough feature of autobiography, presumably on the assumption that verisimilitude must be achieved at all costs, such detail does not necessarily imply a commitment to introspection.

Another dilemma for the student writer that was much in evidence focused around the uncertainty in the writer's tone or in the selection of a persona. The Barneses put it this way: "If their own everyday spoken style and perspectives are not appropriate, where must they look for a voice to assume?" (p. 100). This dilemma is made more acute when pupils are requested to disclose autobiographical details for an audience consisting of a teacher with whom the pupil may or may not be on very good terms. The solutions to this dilemma vary considerably between adopting the aggressive tone and style of everyday speech, and highly poeticized "fine writing" that is aimed, perhaps, at the pupil's perception of the kind of writing that will find most favor in the teacher's eyes.

On the other hand, a more common failing was "a flat lack of expressiveness" (p. 102). The Barneses claim that it is nearly impossible to discover if the inexpressiveness is a defense against the demands of personal writing, or whether it stems from other sources such as a restricted repertoire of rhetorical devices, or from a conscious withdrawal from giving the teacher and the school any more than a minimal effort: The pages are covered with the required amount of writing, but the style is primer and the content negligible.

In addition, the Barneses are highly critical of the extent to which teachers explicitly recommend private/personal topics as a method of ensuring that the students will have at least a handy reservoir of experiences from which to draw. For the Barneses, when "the quality of first-hand experience becomes the measure of all things" (p. 103), it serves to devalue *social* relationships and the worth of other people as well as ignoring public issues that resist this personal approach. This ideology is "Protestant, individual, romantic"; it is "the liberal's dream of transcending his own time" (p. 103). For some students, personal/private writing does provide the chance for them to make sense of their experience within a school curriculum that by and large devalues that experience. But it is clear that perhaps a majority are declining the invitation to open up some of the more vulnerable aspects of their lives on demand. The Barneses go on to ruminate on the value of narrative, that is, fictional, writing as the preferred method of solving these kinds of problems. Although we cannot take up in detail the specifics of their findings on the uses of narrative, a brief comment on their justification for this kind of writing is appropriate in order to prepare the way for our concluding discussion.

The Barneses claim that a paradox lies at the heart of the use of fictional narrative as a way of exploring personal/private topics. Although stories are often told in the first person, they need not be in the least "expressive of the feeling-tone of experience" (p. 104). And it is exactly here that much of the appeal of fictional writing lies for many students—it allows them to deal with things that concern them, or with their fantasy lives, without submitting them directly to public scrutiny. For many students, fiction is a better way of "telling the truth" than the direct narration of personal experiences in auto-biographical discourses like journals. The Barneses themselves offer three further reasons for the appeal of fiction: it "can distance private experience for the self of the narrator"; "popular fiction provides voices and personae that can be easily assumed"; and, because it generally follows a readily understandable sequence, it can provide "an appropriate structure" (p. 104) for those students who have trouble organizing their material.

With this brief sketch now in place, it is time to turn to another part of the Barneses' study, one that deals specifically with what the students themselves said about the kind of writing they were asked to undertake. Of the 157 boys and girls interviewed by the Barneses and their associate, 83 "gave replies explicit enough to be used" (p. 133) when they were questioned about personal writing. Twenty-two girls claimed to enjoy it, while 25 were antagonistic; 10 boys liked it while 26 disliked it. When pressed further to explain their likes and dislikes, the Barneses discovered a diverse range of reasons out of which they tried to abstract attitudes that seemed to cohere. For example, one boy said that you had to have "a poetic gift" (p. 133) to write about yourself or your family; a girl who resisted personal writing thought that English trespassed on things that "you ought to keep to yourself" (p. 133). Some thought that they were too inadequate as persons to be writing about themselves, while others thought that personal writing "sounds like boasting" (p. 133). Although this collection of attitudes was difficult to deal with, the Barneses suggest that there are common motives for students' uneasiness with personal writing: "conflict with sub-cultural values, a desire for privacy, and conflict with some young people's self-images" (p. 133). To overcome these sorts of resistances, many students used fiction as a way of dealing with firsthand experience because it freed them from the likelihood of divulging too much or of coming too close to those areas of experience deemed inappropriate for public (teacher) inspection.

The time has come to consider the general conclusions the Barneses felt it pertinent to draw on the basis of the accumulated evidence summarized here. First of all, the Barneses suggest that owing to the influence of Britton and the London school, there have been drastic changes in teachers' conceptions of the nature of writing that "have generated preconceptions about the relevance of everyday social experience, and placed a high valuation upon the use of writing for self-exploration" (p. 152). But it appears that pupils being prepared for "higher-status" examinations are offered (and select) different writing tasks from those preparing coursework folders for evaluation in "lower-status" examinations. The general point is that different modes of writing present both opportunities and problems; for the personal/autobiographical mode with which we are mainly concerned, some broad comments can be advanced.

To begin with, the autobiographical mode is perceived as more threatening by many pupils. Although it does not draw on the kind of specialized knowledge required to create an argument or to write successfully on some topic of public concern, it does present the problem of selecting an appropriate persona, a problem faced by all would-be autobiographers. Consequently, autobiographical discourse is not a particular favorite of students in the lower streams. Conversely, however, the Barneses discovered that personal/autobiographical writing is often seen as less threatening by those students who come from more middle-class or professional homes and who purportedly bring a greater accumulation of a particular kind of cultural capital. These students were capable of moving easily into a persona that allowed them to deal with personal experience without the risk of overexposing their inner selves. If we are willing to accept these distinctions as provisionally true, then clearly we are dealing with a real mismatch between perceptions of teachers and students. It would appear that teachers are committed to autobiographical writing as a way to have pupils reflect on their own experience, whereas many students find themselves in the position of feeling that this mode is anything but congenial or comfortable for them. This point will be taken up now directly in the concluding section, one that attempts to highlight and critique some of the significant features that have emerged in the course of this chapter. Autobiography as a master discourse promises much; it is the nature of the gap between that promise and its realization that will form the substance of our concluding remarks.

CONCLUSION

I began this chapter with an excursion into the politics of English teaching and the relative positions taken up by the two dominant paradigms: the "literary heritage" or Cambridge school, and the "language" or London school. It was suggested that in spite of instances where they come closer together on some issues than they might be prepared to admit, there are still fundamental political and ideological divisions that keep them at odds. Here is perhaps the moment to say that when they both speak of espousing approaches that center on the needs of the child, they have in mind two different views of who or what that child might be. I have shown that if one wishes to gain a sense of these differences, one might profitably examine their views of autobiography. For if autobiography is recommended on the basis that it provides opportunities for children to reflect on the nature of their experiences as well as to reconstruct a sense of who they are, it could be argued that these ontological and existential aims are honored more in the breach than in the observance. For as the Barneses discovered in their study, those pupils headed for examinations based largely upon their immersion in a literary heritage were offered, but only at one remove, the opportunity to partake of the fruits of self-discovery. On the other hand, pupils headed for lower-status examinations that stressed the accumulation of written work in a folder were invited to submit work that contained evidence of an authentic sense of the personal. To have stated as much this baldly is to have risked oversimplifying the issue by undervaluing the potential for self-discovery that engaging with great literature provides, or to have set too great a store by the examination-driven nature of the English curriculum in the United Kingdom and elsewhere. However, it is apparent to me that it is no accident to find that the emphasis on personal/autobiographical modes of writing is among the first items jettisoned by secondary school teachers who are responsible for ensuring student success in literature-based examinations. Not only do pupils in these classes take away a different sense of what "doing" English consists of, but they are also forcibly made aware that personal experience is valuable only insofar as it can be transformed to add to those deep criteria of style and tone so beloved by teachers and examiners.

But it is well also to acknowledge that the students' brothers and sisters in the bottom sets who are being pressed more forcibly into the autobiographical mode also take away another version of English, one that seems to try too hard to do them good. It is interesting in this connection to note the frequency with which the Barneses encountered teachers using Britton's transactional-expressive-poetic triad to explain and justify their approach to writing. If Britton's ideas have begun to make an inroad into writing instruction, then I would claim that Britton's categories are being invoked by some teachers more as conventional slogans rather than offered in full recognition of pitfalls such as the too-restricted view of the spectator role discussed earlier in connection with the work of Harding. Thus it seems that many teachers are operating on the following premises: If expressive writing is writing that stands close to the pupil's experience, and if provision for personal growth can be made by ensuring that the students are given many opportunities to use expressive writing, then little further thought or justification for using it so widely needs to be given. A prima facie case exists for the normative assumption that if some expressive writing is good, more must be better. So we can see, at least for teachers involved with middle-to-bottom sets of pupils, the nature of the examination is only partly responsible for the heavy emphasis laid on personal/autobiographical modes of writing. Another part of the answer is to be found in the good intentions of teachers who, by employing Britton's ideas as a warrant for their own procedures, have unwittingly appropriated only the more accessible and easily applied aspects of his theory without a corresponding *political* awareness of the manner in which student subjectivities are being constructed in the process (see Silverman, 1980, pp. 126–131).

As we saw from the Barneses' research, a majority of the pupils who were required to work in the autobiographical mode did not particularly enjoy doing so; they solved this dilemma by resorting to other methods which, while they represented milder forms of resistance, were pragmatically motivated to provide the teacher with the kind of writing likely to please, and hence to ensure success. The irony of this situation resides in the fact that the Romantic egalitarian ideology that underpins the London school's language-centered curriculum, and the emancipatory promise in its emphasis on the pupil's personal experience, has been interpreted in ways that have caused many pupils to engage in behavior where the private is kept private, and where what is made public begins to look very much like an anodyne directed at relieving the conscience of the liberal-minded teacher.

A further aspect of the reliance on autobiographical discourse alluded to earlier was the apparent lack of any social dimension to its use. It would seem that, contrary to Dixon's notion of the child's writing as the literature of the classroom, autobiographical writing is in the first place deemed by many as a form of therapy, at the same time as its audience is (naturally enough) the audience-of-one of the teacher. To this end, the keeping of a journal, say, can regress to the level of mere chronology if the often overworked teacher fails to find the time to enter into a dialogue with the student and to gently encourage more risk-taking in the entries. And yet if we apply Britton's thinking to the kinds of real-life situations described by the Barneses in their research, I believe we can make a beginning toward answering the criticism of autobiography's lack of a social dimension, even as we envision an expanded interventionist role for the teacher.

As previously noted, the Barneses discovered that many children disliked personal/autobiographical writing and employed several methods of showing resistance to it. However, what the Barneses also discovered, and what they went on to promote, was the widespread use of fiction as a preferred mode of writing, one that enabled the pupils to write about experience in a nonthreatening way behind any number of fictional personae. But it might be asked whether actively encouraging the writing of fiction is the same thing as Britton's notion of moving children toward the production of artlike performances in their writing. I would contend that it is not. The Barneses' espousal of narrative as a method of self-objectification contains a leap of faith or, less dramatically, an unstated premise regarding the connection between fiction and an author's psyche. It is as though they were saying that an irreducible property of fiction is the inevitability of self-disclosure: the pupil cannot help talking about him- or herself even (or especially) at those moments when the events are most imaginative and made up. Textual production is rarely as overdetermined as this; to consider it so is to leave no room for the *conscious* shaping of experience into the achieved form of art. It is doubtful whether the Barneses would agree with this in quite the terms I have expressed it, but there is a sense in which they conceive of storytelling as a wholly natural activity, one where the pupil already knows the rules from constant exposure to the conventional narratives encountered on TV and in movies, fairy tales, comics, and children's literature. Likewise, many of the teachers interviewed considered it in a similar light. The pedagogical upshot here is a *non*interventionist one: encourage narrative writing, lots of it; do not make the students too uncomfortable about their writing; and believe that this is the way to make provision for the exploration of the self that is the goal of these narrative opportunities.

On the other hand, if I read Britton correctly, he considers that the artlike performances of pupils' narratives display some of the skills of the real artist. But it is equally clear to me that a large part of Britton's mandate for teachers is to have them show pupils how to move progressively away from the naive production of narrative toward the more consciously conceived and executed literary artifact. This movement not only serves to explore the idea of a unitary self already constituted in various ways, but also encourages the construction of a number of literary selves as a way of bringing together and reflecting upon the influence of culture on identity. And notice, too, that it is not so much in the successful achievement of a literary artifact that the greatest payoff will come in terms of the child's objectification of self and circumstances, but rather in the cognitive and affective operations involved when the pupil goes to work shaping experience *by taking on the role of the artist*. The raw material is still the pupil's personal experience, the pupil's autobiographical facts, if you will; the method and role, however, are clearly that of the artist as spectator of the self in action, distanced from the art and making decisions about the nature of the public presentation of that self. It is worth repeating, however, that this aesthetic project does not proceed from "the essentialist position that humans have a simple, purposive nature" (Lanham, 1976, p. 36), but rests on a view of identity where by means of language individuals can make and remake themselves within society. It is this that is the logical import of Britton's thinking on both narrative and the place of autobiographical discourse within it. To conceive of it in this way is to visualize an expanded role for the teacher, who, if he or she begins from the belief that the closer autobiography approaches the condition of art the closer it is to fiction, can begin to provide examples in reading and writing of the range of effects possible in first- and third-person narration. In other words, the pupil must be given the opportunity to follow a progressive course in conventional and experimental writing techniques whereby private experience stands a greater chance of being transformed into the public symbolism of art. Then the students' narratives could truly become the literature of the classroom at the same time as the child learns something about the role of the artist as licensed liar, and about the constructed nature of the fictions we variously call self, society, and reality.

5 Remembering Ourselves at School: Autobiography and Teacher Education

Education in the limited form of schooling can thus be interpreted as a systematic flight from existence; *an attempt to blot out the dirty smudge of the self so as to secure "pure objectivity" and "final neutrality."*

Peter Abbs, 1979

Whatever else the Barneses' research uncovered for us in the previous chapter, it is evident that there exists in the minds of many teachers a substantial gulf between the persuasiveness or applicability of a theorist like Britton, and the pressures and constraints experienced in the world of practice. In like manner, students—who are being prepared in the United Kingdom and elsewhere to write what are widely perceived as lower-status external examinations—are often ambivalent, or display overt signs of resistance, to teacher requests to write about the kinds of experiences that many students consider inappropriate for public (teacher) consumption. On the face of it, then, it might be argued that there are some deep divisions between, on the one hand, theories espoused by teachers and the actualities of their practice, and on the other, between a student's need to display the self for grades and the need to erect some barriers to keep more sensitive areas of private experience at a safe distance from public scrutiny. In addition, this conflict is further exacerbated to the extent that Britton's solution for placing language education programs on new epistemological and moral foundations is offered in direct opposition to state-run systems of examinations, which would seem to privilege a version of English derived from a different epistemology and a different

96

conception of the relationship between knowledge and power. It would also seem that a commitment to provide opportunities for students to write the self by constructing narratives of personal experience is largely the function of the elementary or primary grades of schooling, a commitment that is hastily (and gratefully) dropped by teachers under the academic pressures of secondary school, or shunted into the lower tracks where its therapeutic potential is engaged as it is pressed into service to facilitate the adjustment of certain kinds of students to society.

The political implications of this scenario for literacy education are plain to see as soon as we recognize that, as Chapter 4 indicated, the field itself has been riven into conflicting factions. There are those who would hold fast to some version of the familiar Deweyan project whereby, as Abbs (1977) states, "To teach English is to seek the elucidation and celebration of the self through the art of symbolization" (p. 56), and those who would perceive themselves as more realistic or useful in that their version of English takes full account of the wishes of most parents, who want their children to be successful in the race for places in tertiary education, or for an entrée into better-paying jobs. Of course, the conflict is more complex than this sketch would make it appear, since we would at least want to ask whether each position necessarily excluded the possibility of achieving both its own and the other's stated goals, or whether the conflict was so profound that nothing less than a struggle over competing visions for society was at stake. Of course these questions cannot be resolved here; what is apparent, however, and what our present excursion into teacher education will undoubtedly show, is that if many of the claims Britton wants to make regarding the centrality of autobiography for language education are ever going to catch on seriously, then some important changes will have to be made in the way in which language education teachers are trained, as well as in the kinds of theories and arguments in-service and graduate students in language education are exposed to.

To this point I have resisted calling this state of affairs a crisis, since crisis has been used so often in situations where a dramatic note is required that we have largely become anesthetized to its tendencies to startle and shock. However, to the extent that poetic or artistic avenues to the discovery of truth can be seen as part of the legacy of Romanticism, where art promises immediate knowledge free from the killing procedures of scientific analysis and method (Wordsworth's "we murder to dissect"), a neo-Romantic project like Britton's, if not directly responsible for precipitating a crisis within language education, may be one of the most powerful expressions of a more general sense that the status of knowledge itself has entered a critical phase. In this sense, the educational crisis, to which some teacher-educators have offered the turn to autobiography as one vital element of a solution, has stemmed from an epistemological crisis, a crisis that, according to Burns (1982, p. 85), has affected not only the way we conceptualize knowledge, but many "socio-cultural processes including the definition of the individual" as well. Thus, the educators whose work we shall be bringing forward for inspection in this chapter can usefully be seen as those who would also agree in principle with Britton, and whose vision for teacher education would accord well with Britton's hopes for language education. The extent to which autobiography is justified by these individuals not only as a means of fulfilling many of the hopes for reconstituted teacher education programs but as an ideal vehicle for problematizing the nature of knowledge itself will become apparent in due course. What needs to be clarified briefly in this introductory section is the trend toward that changing view of knowledge itself and what this might signify for a way of rethinking teacher education and the place of autobiography within it.

THE CRISIS OF KNOWLEDGE

Although it is hazardous to begin with a series of generalizations, we may note with some confidence that the long-established paradigm and tradition of empirical research that undergirds the social sciences have come increasingly under fire. As the validity and meaning of its empirical tools have been questioned, as well as the value neutrality of some research itself, other paradigms that developed out of hermeneutics and critical theory have been concerned with concentrating on the *meaning* of the research and on the interpretive elements that adhere to any discussion of research findings (Hekman, 1986; Van Manen, 1990). Certainly it would be wrong to claim that the empirical paradigm has collapsed, for as we will see later its attractions can still enthrall even the most committed qualitative researcher; what needs to be stressed is that as the empirical paradigm begins to feel the encroachment from other paradigms, how can this impact also make itself felt in teacher education? I frame the question in this way because to ask how it has impacted teacher education would be to request empirical verification for which there is at this moment no extensive evidence. It would also ignore the importance of Hopkins's (1985) drift theory of organizational change in teacher education. Under this theory, any external pressure for change is moderated through the "saga" (p. 127) of each particular institution and hence is essentially unpredictable. In other words, regardless of how knowledge has been problematized, teacher education is still by and large perceived as a time where selected research findings and quickly transmissible skills are purveyed to would-be teachers in advance of their practicum in the schools.

Nevertheless, what I am after here is to inquire into what, if any, is the relationship between the epistemology that the teacher-educators in this chapter are turning against, and the privileging of autobiography as a model of the knowledge that they are arguing for. The importance of this for teacher education is evident. If there has been some erosion in the widespread confidence in the scientific model of knowledge creation in general, then to fail to find a place for alternative models in the education of teachers is no less than a dereliction of responsibility, even in the face of drift theories of change and the substantial inertia within institutions for changing the status quo. It is precisely this point that the reformers under discussion would agree with and where the turn to autobiography enters the picture.

As we will see, none of these teacher-educators shrinks from leveling criticism at current practices, practices that they believe are responsible for the lowly status of teacher education in general and that continue to place teacher education in a reactive position. By reactive they mean that teacher education is placed in the position of waiting for the findings from empirically validated studies in order to make decisions about what to do next. Such a position implies a view of the relationship between theory and practice that McKeon (1951) called *logistic;* that is, that research findings are or ought to be directly (and immediately) applicable to the world of practice. As an alternative, one that will allow teachers to become active in knowledge generation and that reconceptualizes the theory/practice relationship more in terms of what McKeon went on to call the *dialectical* and *problematic* models, autobiography is offered as a research method, one grounded in the premises and practices of phenomenology. Although autobiography as a research method used by figures like Butt and Raymond is controversial and can be easily attacked for its lack of rigor, subjectivity, and lack of replicability, its proponents continue to cling to the central notion that such attacks derive from an alternative view of knowledge creation, one that ignores the personal, situated, and existential bases of *all* knowledge.

This kind of conflict takes us close to questioning the vision we have for the institutional training of future generations of teachers, and more urgently poses in a new way questions regarding the purpose and direction of education itself. And, as the following discussion will make apparent, the small but growing number of teacher-educators who have moved toward autobiography are pinning their hopes for education on a position that stems not only from an alternative epistemology, but that sees society and culture as a battlefield where the mind-numbing forces of mass media and their scientific and technological cohorts have all but wiped out the ability of individuals to determine the course and shape of their own lives. It should come as no surprise, therefore, that the evangelical, redemptive purpose of such a project should have discovered in autobiography the perfect vehicle for restoring a lost sense of self and for reminding us that education in its widest conception always entails a vision of the future.

As we move, then, to a more searching discussion of the place these writers would make for autobiography in basic and ongoing teacher education, several points must be kept in mind. First, the arguments, points of view, and practices advanced by each of these writers represent only the voice of a minority, and anything resembling the large-scale restructuring of teacher education along the lines they suggest seems a long way off, if it indeed ever will take place. Second, as one might expect, all four writers share a great deal in common with respect to a central core of assumptions about the status of knowledge, the position of the individual, and the characteristics of an ideal teacher education program. One writer in particular, Madeleine Grumet (1981), has gone even further and has advanced autobiography as a method for theorizing about the curriculum; consequently, more time will be devoted to this aspect of her thinking on autobiography in the next chapter. For now, only those aspects of her theory and practice regarding teacher education courses will occupy our attention to the extent that they differ from or augment those of the three other figures. Third, and last, this chapter will provide a further opportunity for testing how our developing notions of autobiography stand up as a way of providing a basis for critique. With this in mind, we turn now to the work of Peter Abbs in England, Madeleine Grumet in the United States, and Richard Butt and Danielle Raymond in Canada.

AUTOBIOGRAPHY IN TEACHER EDUCATION:
BRITISH, AMERICAN, AND CANADIAN PERSPECTIVES

The Preservice Teacher as Artist

Abbs (1976) begins his criticism of current practices in teacher education in typically dramatic fashion: "Colleges of Education are now facing a crisis of meaning" (p. 120). The crisis not only signifies a need to rethink the place and function of colleges of education, but connotes above all a need to discuss "the true ideals of education in a rapidly emerging technocratic society" (p. 120). As we will see, for Abbs one villain of his story of contemporary society is always the mass media in their many manifestations, what Abbs (1976, p. 77) calls "the counterfeit culture." And it is against this counterfeit culture that we must all be prepared to struggle, especially our children, who are (supposedly) more susceptible to mistaking the shadow-pictures constructed by the media for the true form of reality itself.

But if Platonic metaphors are appropriate in one sense, in another they are inadequate to capture what for Abbs is nothing less than the Manichean struggle between the good forces of education and the evil forces of mass and crass culture. In this Abbs remains true to his training as a student of F. R. Leavis, and to the view of mass culture promulgated by figures like Denys Thompson, who, as we saw in the previous chapter, argued strenuously for an education system that would educate students against those forces that make for conformity and unthinking acceptance of reality in its taken-for-granted aspects. And where better to begin to stem the tide of this powerful influence on our lives than in colleges of education, where teachers (and in particular teachers of English) can be trained not only for the missionary work involved in becoming what Mathieson (1975) has called "preachers of culture," but also for the work of restoring in our students lost sources of personal creativity that have been buried under the sedimented weight of those pressures that make for inauthentic and stunted lives?

But although Abbs has continued to bear the standard for the place of the arts and the expressive disciplines generally within education, he has also returned on many occasions to the philosophy of existentialism as a view that is less "an enclosed and explanatory system" than a way of pointing "unambiguously to the dramatic and dynamic nature of existence" (1979, p. 97). According to Abbs, an appreciation for some of the key tenets of existentialism incurs consequences for education that far outweigh the apparent gloominess and pessimism of many of its more famous documents and proponents. One immediate reason for this is that to adopt an existential framework for education ensures that we keep constantly in front of us "the essential biographical element in human knowledge" (Abbs, 1977, p. 127). To do so means to turn away from seeing knowledge as broken up into the self-contained units of subjects or disciplines, and also to turn away from assuming that learning consists of such typical activities as memorizing and recording. The function of schools of education under this scenario would be clear enough: it would be to offer a "radically different concept of education from that which the students have come to accept as normal" (1976, p. 123).

However, for Abbs there is more involved in an existential approach to education than this. Working from the etymology of the word *existence*, "to stand out, to emerge, to become visible" (1979, p. 97), to exist then means to stand out from our surroundings to become a particular person. From this premise, men or women cannot be said to truly exist until they begin to step out from the pressures exerted by their backgrounds—class, family, culture, country—and take on the task of shaping their own lives. For Abbs (1979) this existential project is, as has been mentioned many times, an essentially artistic process, one that returns to individuals the responsibility of becoming their own artist and of preempting all those other forces that are working to disguise the extent of their freedom. It is this idea that unites all existential philosophers and philosophies, whether of a Marxist, Christian, or other variety, namely, "that the human world can exist only in and through the consciousness of individuals" (Abbs, 1979, p. 98).

One immediate consequence of placing an emphasis on the consciousness of the individual is to realize that there can be no knowledge without a knower. But it also means that if knowledge can only be within consciousness, then it is subject to the vagaries of consciousness, all those fluctuating states and fallibilities with which we are all familiar. For Abbs, this fact points not only to rejecting the idea that knowledge is something "out there," something there to be assimilated by a knower, but also that it compels us to see that knowledge is always contextualized, part of quite specific relationships, cultures, and situations. In other words, what Abbs (1979) is arguing for is a more integrated concept of humanity's search for meaning, one that moves *from the inside out*, or, as he puts it, "an unfolding and progressive articulation of the self in relationship to the world which surrounded it" (p. 112). It is in this forward movement, a wholly engaging process characterized by the shifts in our struggle to give meaning to our lives rather than by setting one's sights on an explicit end, that Abbs finds the distinguishing marks of education. This would certainly accord well not only with Dewey's and his collaborator Bentley's view of education and knowledge (1949), and in particular that aspect which views education as essentially an aesthetic project, but also would account for Abbs's concern with reconceiving of teacher education in a way diametrically opposed to the philosophy of Facts satirized by Dickens in his portrait of Gradgrind in *Hard Times*. Abbs's aesthetic concept of education relocates attention on the learner as a maker, an artist; hence, education is not something that one is given in the sense of "receiving" a good education, but rather is an active undertaking involving "the continuous effort to re-create myself within the context in which I exist" (Abbs, 1979, p. 111).

Under this existential approach to education, certain consequences follow that are of supreme importance for reconceptualizing the role of the teacher, as well as for reshaping an approach to schools and classrooms as sites where knowledge is created. Interestingly, one immediate consequence is for Abbs to turn to the phenomenological potential in autobiography so that teachers in training can begin by considering their own educational experiences and then move outward toward a kind of collective interpretation of those experiences. Abbs is aware of the apparent anomaly here in that he has been discussing education all along in terms of individuals and creative processes as if in isolation from other individuals engaged in the same undertaking. He (1979) counters by stating, "Yet following in the wake of Martin Buber's philosophy, I suspect, paradoxically, this [education] can only be realized through the power of relationships and the power of community" (p. 118). The phenomenological project of teachers in training as a community of interpreters, then, is to begin to peel away the layers of meaning that different interpretations can bring to a description of an experience so that slowly a "complex, composite picture of whoever or whatever is being studied (it may be an individual child, a class of children, a school, a family, a factory, an office, a small community) is built up" (Abbs, 1976, p. 131).

This collaborative effort at the interpretation of educational experience is not undertaken without some awareness as to the risks involved; therefore, to virtually every detail of his description of the use of autobiography Abbs appends words like "slowly," "sensitively," and "delicately" as forceful reminders for instructors and participants alike as to the importance of building a reservoir of trust. The following quotation will provide not only some sense of the autobiographical method but also of the sensitivity that for Abbs should at all times be present:

> The different individual responses to various teachers, types of school, subject-matter as revealed in the various autobiographies could be compared and, through a delicate process of collaboration initiated by the tutor, evaluated. Recent ideas about social class, about language codes, about play, competition, learning, symbolism, could be slowly introduced and discussed where they clarify the particular experience in question. (Abbs, 1976, p. 133)

In addition to maintaining an awareness of the need to exercise great care in the interpretive process, Abbs frequently turns to the testimony of the classic literary autobiographies themselves, apparently in order to discover their special characteristics and to find there a means of approaching elements in his own students' autobiographies. One must assume this is the case, since he never overtly states a reason for alluding to so many famous autobiographies (his distressingly all-male reading list includes Augustine, Rousseau, Goethe, Wordsworth, Mill, Gosse, Ruskin, Trollope, Tolstoy, and Gorki, but not Martineau, Woolf, Nin, McCarthy, or Kingston), nor does he at any time formally acknowledge that autobiography is essentially a fictional undertaking. Although one might be prepared to concede that, for Abbs, this point may have been too obvious to mention, it is nevertheless a startling omission, especially when one considers his own literary training and the enormous lengths he takes to deal fairly with the autobiographer's use of time, memory, experience, metaphor, and symbol. What are we to make, for example, of Abbs's account and response to the following anecdote he relates regarding a conversation with a student who was experiencing difficulty beginning her autobiography?

> "Does it have to be personal?"
> "How do you mean?" I asked.
> "I mean written in the first person," she said.
> "Gorki's autobiography was written in the third person," I answered.
> That was enough. . . . The student had suddenly found that she could best capture her childhood by employing a third-person narrative. For some reason, an impersonal method of writing released her imagination and freed her memory which until then had been constricted by the direct first-person presentation we normally associate with autobiography. (1976, p. 162)

Certainly there is little doubt that on one level a number of readers' expectations are set up when a discourse announces itself as an autobiography, not the least of which is that the person's life story will normally be narrated using the first-person pronoun as part of what Lejeune (1975, 1989) has called *le pacte autobiographique.* It is as though choosing to write in the first person not only guarantees the authenticity of the facts related in the text, as well as guaranteeing that the "I" of the discourse corresponds to the name on the cover of the book, but that the writer is willing to stand behind and take responsibility for the truth and accuracy of the facts contained in the account. However, when the third-person, omniscient narrator is selected as the preferred method of narration, much more is involved than Abbs seems prepared to admit. It is not only a more impersonal method of narration, one that releases a writer from the constrictions of the first person, but omniscient narration announces itself at every turn as perhaps *the* distinguishing mark of a particular kind of narrative fiction. Abbs completely blurs this distinction and with it the kind of criteria one might adopt when attempting to interpret and ascertain the truth-claims implied in his students' narratives. For Abbs, the selection by students of either first- or third-person narrative techniques is directly related to the kinds of experiences the students wanted to write about. For some, the third person was used to describe "more harrowing experiences" (1976, p. 162), while for others the first person was used to evoke "more leisurely and happy moments" (p. 162).

Now while we would definitely want to afford students the opportunity of experimenting with different narrative techniques, many might wish to question the wisdom of proceeding, as Abbs appears to do, from the position of believing that the selection of point of view in the long run makes little difference to how we should read or interpret the students' narratives. In other words, Abbs tries to remove from the agenda the interpretive problems involved in approaching autobiographies composed from either a first- or third-person point of view, and instead chooses to emphasize the student's right to select whatever form or style desired that will express his or her attitude toward the chosen experience. This sort of approach, although laudable, fails to move much beyond a naive realist's approach to the relationship between the writing subject and the experience written about. Abbs seems unwilling to let go of his belief in the correspondence between the actual words of the student's autobiography and the experiences and incidents to which they refer. Language, to him, is apparently a transparent medium that can be employed entirely referentially without any intervening "noise" or distortion accumulated by the act of writing itself.

Abbs's autobiographical project to make the private public is, as we have seen, admirable insofar as he understands the sensitive nature of the undertaking, its ethical dimensions, its essentially collaborative aspects, and the delicate role of the instructor. In addition, he makes a strong case on both philosophical and educational grounds for subscribing to an existential and phenomenological approach to education and knowledge that stands in opposition to teacher training institutions, which continue to rely on a simplistic view of what the relationship between educational research and practice ought to be. Furthermore, we may credit him with realizing that the study of classic autobiographies could play an important role in confirming a student's sense of self by demonstrating how the path to self-realization is always a site of tension, discontinuity, and struggle, yet one in which moments of transcendence can still be found.

And yet at the same time what has also been clearly demonstrated is an unwillingness or recalcitrance to admit or to follow through on the insights gained from his academic study of autobiography. Although Abbs's studies brought to the fore a deep appreciation for its status as a fictional genre, he has clearly declined to bring different methods of literary interpretation to the discussion of the students' autobiographies themselves. If he had, this process might have lead him to consider more fully, for example, the rhetorical elements in autobiography as a linguistic construction or as an example of Hart's (1970) drama of fluctuating intentions. Neither of these is taken up at all by Abbs, with the result that the excerpts from his students' autobiographies that he so lovingly quotes on so many occasions are allowed to pass without any searching criticisms being brought to bear on them as crafted literary productions. These silences in Abbs's work begin to resound with increasing force even in spite of other aspects of his argument that are persuasive and powerful. By turning now to a brief inspection of Grumet's work in the United States, perhaps we can form a clearer notion of what an autobiographical method that consciously proceeds from an acknowledgment of its fictional nature might look like.

Autobiography and Dialectical Pedagogy

A major section in the last chapter of Pinar and Grumet's *Toward a Poor Curriculum* (1976), a work that will receive more extended treatment in the next chapter, is given over to a description by Grumet of her experience in a teacher training seminar at the University of Rochester. The seminar proceeded from an intensive scrutiny of what Grumet (1976d) labels "the subjective" (p. 148). In practice this meant that autobiography would be used in order to examine the students' educational experiences as well as "the assumptions that they would bring with them into their classrooms" (p. 148). Grumet's description of the seminar is an intensely moving piece of phenomenological writing itself, evoking for the reader the feeling that we ourselves are taking part in the seminar and sharing its hesitancies, tensions, transferences, and exhilarations. Although comparisons are often difficult, we can at least see that the distance between Abbs's description of his own course and Grumet's often disturbing document *as autobiographical accounts of educational experience themselves* is so significant that their divergence at crucial moments provides a rare opportunity for us to focus attention on the realities of working with autobiography within teacher training institutions, and to meditate briefly on a number of important issues, of which the role of the instructor is only a more obvious example.

What should also emerge from this discussion are the kinds of reservations and criticisms that seem likely to follow the institutional use of autobiography and whose existence might tend to lessen its chances of being adopted more widely as a basis for teacher education. Consequently, I shall be concerned here with highlighting only those elements of Grumet's practice that stand in contrast to Abbs's own, or that themselves raise the possibility of being open to question in a number of ways.

First of all, Grumet's course is radical in the sense that it eschews the lesson-plan-and-teaching-gimmick format of traditional methods courses in favor of autobiographical work that is developed on three levels: discussion, writing, and theater. Grumet is well aware that to undertake such a course is also to incur "the Dean's outrage [and] the snickering of faculty" (p. 150), and in effect calls her own moral courage and beliefs into question. In addition, of course, it is certain to incur the suspicion and resistance of the students, many or most of whom are more concerned with learning the gimmicks than they are with exploring what seem to them some dubious paths to enlightenment or self-knowledge. These feelings of resistance and of impatience with the course's direct lack of applicability remained continually on some students' agendas, and it is clear that whatever successes Grumet experienced were largely due to the considerable force of her own personality, a point to which we will return later.

A major aspect of the course was the use of theater exercises as warm-up activities in order for the students to explore alternative avenues of self-discovery and expression. As can be imagined, for many these exercises were uncomfortable, especially exercises designed to have the students look at each other directly and establish eye contact. Grumet talked with the group briefly about the purpose of these exercises, not in order for the discussion to become an encounter session but to stress that the information made available from these exercises should be gathered from their own private response to the experience rather than from the reactions of others in the group. Grumet was reluctant to spend time "verbalizing non verbal work" (p. 153), especially when she realized that some students were resisting it and could see little immediate connection to the world of teaching. The same could not be said for the more formal study of autobiography (significantly, Sartre's *Words* rather than one of the texts on Abbs's list) and for an excursion into Olney's theory of autobiography in his *Metaphors of Self* (1972). This more traditional approach, where students could discuss something objective like a theory or a text, was of course more comfortable and provided an opportunity for Grumet herself to air her own reasons for basing the course on autobiography.

In this respect, then, Grumet's autobiographical project involved both theoretical and practical elements, and was responsible for creating moments when the students could question (and some in a very hostile manner) the reasons for undertaking those specific tasks and assignments. What comes across in Grumet's description of these often tense and troublesome group discussions is a concern to work with and through her own tendency to adopt a defensive posture so that, as the skilled therapist does, the currents of hostility could be turned to everyone's advantage. As she states, "We used the discussions of autobiography not only to develop our understanding of the genre, but to illustrate and examine pedagogical practice as well" (p. 155).

In addition, when it came to students actually writing their autobiographies, Grumet goes one step further than Abbs and engages in a written dialogue with each student, numbering the places in their texts to which she wants to respond and writing her own comments on a separate piece of paper. Whereas Abbs provided us with examples of his students' work that exhibited a great deal of writing skill and that may indeed have represented the students' first draft attempts, Grumet's examples range from very stiff and formal early productions to the more fluent and considered efforts that emerged in response to Grumet's (and other students') comments. There is little doubt that Grumet shows her own considerable skill as a writer and as a sensitive respondent here; what is also apparent is that as the students rewrote their initial essays and exchanged them with each other, the locus of evaluation and power began to shift in subtle but perceptible ways in the class, to the extent that Grumet's hope that the students would provide "both the thesis and antithesis for themselves" (p. 160) began to assume more palpable shape.

To encourage this dialogical relationship further, the students rewrote a paragraph of their essays completely, "reversing every assertion, conviction, interpretation it expressed" (p. 160). These paragraphs were then read aloud to demonstrate that there were indeed truths in each version that also provided moments for self-discovery and reflection. And as the students' subsequent efforts began to show the marks of greater engagement as well as a "growing tolerance for ambiguity" (p. 162), in many cases linear narration was given up and experiments were made in other ways of narrating in order to examine the educational experience from different angles, to turn it around and look at it from another perspective.

As the course progressed and as students left the confines of the university for their periods of observation and practice in the schools, the classes met less frequently, and the more formal writing of autobiography was replaced with more informal journal-keeping and short descriptive pieces. The course drew to a close with statements from the students regarding their experience of the course, as well as a concluding statement from Grumet herself. Significantly, the issue of trust loomed large over this wrap-up session, and even as Grumet herself admits in her paper that she found the students' comments useful and that many acknowledged how the course had indeed helped them, the weariness creeps into her own tone as she sums up: "Perhaps it is too much to ask for trust, too much of an intrusion, I'd settle for a laying aside of distrust, but even that may be too ambitious" (p. 169).

Among the many issues this exposition of Grumet's work serves to raise, three stand out as worthy of particular attention, especially in the light of our earlier discussion of Abbs's own theory and practice. For many critics of the autobiographical approach to teacher education, I am certain these issues alone would be sufficient to cast serious doubts upon its feasibility regardless of the sophistication of the project's theoretical underpinnings. Nor do I at this point wish to be drawn into a position that would seem to favor one side or the other; rather, the criticisms offered now must be seen as part of the larger effort to clarify the claims that are being made on autobiography's behalf, as well as part of the attempt to square these claims and aspirations with the kind of realities and pressures that would prevent the widespread restructuring of teacher education along the lines mapped out by Abbs and Grumet.

First of all, we must consider the role and personality of the instructor. It is abundantly clear that no matter what steps are taken by the instructor, for example, from Grumet's selection of clothing and seating herself among the students (1976d, pp. 147–48) to Abbs's use of different media for having the students explore various methods of self-representation (1976, pp. 136–37), the issue of power is always at or near the surface of things. As Grumet (1976d) reports, one of her students could not suspend his awareness "that the person responding to his essays, requesting theatre work free of editing self-consciousness was also the same person who would be observing his work in schools for certification and giving him grades in the course" (p. 169). Not only is this a problem, but the trust that Abbs claims is fundamental to any use of autobiography could be early and permanently undermined by the same kind of personality conflicts that often characterize any classroom encounter, in which a familiar student tactic is to "read" the instructor and then provide the kind of work that is sure to find favor.

But even if some methods could be found to minimize the deleterious effects of the unequal power relations, ironically, the question remains regarding the training and preparation of the instructors themselves. Not only would they have to be proficient in a wide array of expressive, theatrical techniques, but also expert in the difficult skill of the nondirective (Rogerian) psychotherapist. Clearly the role Grumet envisions for the instructor may be said to surpass some commonly held boundaries that often provide what is thought of as a necessary and saving distance between teacher and taught. In other words, it is a far cry from being persuaded by an argument that the existential approach to education put forward by Abbs and Grumet is valid on its own terms, to accumulating the repertoire of techniques and personal characteristics essential to bringing such a course into being. Certainly the dialectical interplay between tension and cooperation is a feature of any course or classroom; in this sense, then, Grumet's course is no worse and may perhaps be somewhat better than its more traditional counterparts. What is crucial, however, is the fact that when the instructor's agenda becomes of necessity the student's agenda, then it is small wonder that the use of autobiography, predicated as it is upon public self-revelation, is met with resistances that often remain unresolved throughout the duration of the course. This is not to argue against Grumet's attempt, but rather to keep before us the possibility of a law of diminishing returns as instructors considering a move to autobiography calculate the availability of net educational gains when the amount of aggravation and distrust is divided by their uncertainty as to a satisfactory outcome for the majority of students.

Second, both Abbs and Grumet spend much time discussing the responses of the students, either as they emerge during the course or immediately upon completion. Indeed, the section that follows Grumet's essay in the final chapter of Pinar and Grumet's book is a retrospective account by one of their teacher/assistants comparing this course with the more traditional education methods course he had completed during his own training year. It is unnecessary to pursue the specifics of his response; what is important is that he is not only willing to admit that most students reacted in a hostile manner to the course, but that, ironically, this response is and ought to be a permanent feature of any course that relies on autobiography. By coming to realize this, he himself gained insight into his role as an instructor, namely, that he could "no longer be satisfied [being] a passive or private footbridge" (1976d, p. 173), but that he would have to "shake up assumptions and disallow facile compliance" (p. 173). For him, agitation and resistance are not something to be regretted, as Grumet herself appears to do; rather, the instructor should welcome the agitation since it "initiates the dialectical process" (p. 173) and causes students to "construct their own existential meanings" (p. 174). From this testimony, then, we may deduce that it will indeed require an extraordinary commitment on the part of the instructor, a corresponding fund of unlimited energy, and a secure ego in order even to begin dealing with the convoluted dynamic that apparently is a procedural commonplace of the autobiographical method.

On the other hand, whether owing to personal modesty or the profound socialization of British students, nowhere in Abbs's description do we hear anything remotely resembling expressions of student resistance or the beginnings of conflict. What Grumet had agonized over, Abbs deals with in two sentences: "The tutor can suggest possibilities but he cannot and should not seek to solve the student's dilemmas. And the student must at all times remain free to reject the proferred suggestions" (1976d, pp. 161–62). The recognition by Abbs of deep conflict and resistance on the part of the students, as well as the strenuous demands made on the instructor, seems never to surface, and is smoothed over in what one can only take to be a deliberate rhetorical ploy on his part in order to accentuate the elements of the course that will support his overall argument.

Third, and last, lest the impression be given that a teacher education course based on autobiography is nothing more than a running battle between students and instructor, it is abundantly clear that a considerable number of significant outcomes resulted from both Abbs's and Grumet's courses. This point will be taken up again in the concluding section; for now I will deal with only one aspect that is of immediate interest, an aspect that needs to be considered and accounted for. This is the pervading sense within many students that they have, in writing their autobiographies, experienced a revelation or epiphany of a distinctly spiritual or religious kind. Whether this revelation is experienced by one of Abbs's students into the contrast between how harshly a teacher treated him and how ingratiatingly obsequious that teacher was to the student's parents (1976d, p. 152), or by one of Grumet's students into his need to move away from farm life in order to grow as a person (1976d, p. 159), these feelings of a profound sense of release appear to constitute a cross-cultural phenomenon. Significantly, Abbs discovers one plausible explanation for this recurring phenomenon in William James's discussion of St. Augustine in his *Varieties of Religious Experience*, especially James's distinction between "first-born" and "twice-born" persons. First-born persons "are born with an inner constitution which is harmonious and well-balanced from the outset" (Abbs, 1976, p. 159), whereas the existence of twice-born persons "is little more than a series of zigzags, as now one tendency and now another gets the upper hand" (p. 160). James found the perfect example of this divided self in St. Augustine; Abbs finds in St. Augustine a perfect example of existential man, one constantly prey to irrationality but also driven by a longing for transcendence. Clearly for Abbs, and consistent with a view of autobiography that emerged in Chapter 2, man's inner being is a battleground between an actual and an ideal self; the writing of autobiography moves an individual some way toward creating that ideal self, at the same time as it heals those divisions and provides sources of insight into both self and others. It is not surprising, then, to discover that Abbs's and Grumet's students partake in the fruits of this spiritual endeavor as well; this would account for the continuous expressions of surprise and delight in their writings as new attitudes are adopted and as hidden feelings stand revealed.

To this point in our discussion of the advantages and liabilities of using autobiography in teacher education, the work of Abbs and Grumet has allowed us to focus on its use with pre-service teachers. The work of Richard Butt and his collaborator Danielle Raymond in Canada (1987, 1989), although largely concerned at present with its use in graduate education as an adjunct to the project in personal practical knowledge initiated by Connelly and Clandinin (Clandinin, 1985, 1986; Connelly & Clandinin, 1987), makes some claims for autobiographical inquiry as a method of research. What is of interest here, and what will assist in augmenting our general appreciation for the place of autobiography, is to inspect those claims. Not only do Butt and Raymond (1989) subscribe fully to Grumet's aim of providing teachers in training with a way of critically assessing their educational experience, but what they term collaborative autobiography can be used in research with experienced teachers into teaching for the purpose of examining "the evolution of individual ways of thinking and acting in the classroom, notably how teachers continue to learn and develop their own particular knowledge" (p. 406).

Autobiographical Inquiry as Research

As we noted at the beginning of this chapter, the existence of qualitative research methods within the social sciences has resulted in the general recognition of its interpretive nature. Regardless of this recognition, however, for Butt and Raymond (1989) autobiographical research still "remains controversial in the light of the nature of the research process and data" (p. 413). As we will see, Butt and Raymond offer collaborative autobiography as a methodology that they claim has been constructed to offset the problems in individual autobiography surrounding the use of biased or incomplete data. Before inspecting this claim further, it will be useful to examine briefly their statements on this matter from the perspectives on autobiography made available by literary theory that we discussed in Chapter 2.

It is certain that a researcher committed to a quantitative paradigm would rule the data disclosed by autobiographical narratives immediately out of court. And it is precisely here that Butt and Raymond realize the controversial status of their data, and yet the list they construct of the manifold ways in which autobiographical data are necessarily incomplete are the very reasons others have given for turning toward autobiography in the first place. Certainly we can agree with Butt and Raymond that autobiography reveals "personal bias and selective recall"; certainly autobiography shapes "stories according to dispositions"; certainly autobiographers "create coherence, perhaps, where there are cracks, flaws and problems"; and certainly in the process of making the unconscious conscious we "reshape the nature of how experiences are known and understood" (p. 413). However, we might wish to probe Butt and Raymond's con-

tention that even if autobiography creates "new meaning," that its
inward-looking nature is essentially "narcissistic and solipsistic" (p.
413). It would appear that Butt and Raymond are committed from the
outset to a view of language as a transparent medium and consequently consider that the value of a narrative account lies primarily in
the extent to which it can be checked out for its correspondence to
some previous event. In other words, Butt and Raymond seem to
want an autobiographical narrative to resemble a window that provides access to some preexisting reality uncontaminated by the writing process and the intentions of the writer.

•   That these researchers should be concerned, from a scientific
point of view, with the problem of validity is understandable. However, their desire to generalize from specific cases by attempting to set
up criteria tests for group membership as in prosopography (Stone,
1972) leaves open to question the possibility of ever pinning down the
messy, slippery, incomplete, and selective data of autobiographical
narratives as an inductive basis for scientific generalizations. Butt and
Raymond's (1989) solution to this problem is their espousal of collaborative autobiography.

Basically the process of collaborative autobiography entails, not
as one might expect a method of coauthorship, but rather being exposed to other individual teachers' stories as an aid to memory, and
to the kinds of questions that might attend a discussion of those stories. To belong to a group given over to narrating autobiographical
accounts of teaching is thought to "prod the edges and blank spaces
of our selective recall and repression of certain areas" (p. 414). Other
teachers' stories act as counterbiographies, different ways of seeing
similar contexts, and ensure that our own stories are grounded in current reality as well as holding in check the entropic tendency to "over
fictionalize" (p. 414). This group process, constructed and based on
shared feelings of trust, encourages us "to unmask ourselves" so that
teachers come to reveal "personal flaws" (p. 414) and to assume responsibility for their own stories. Significantly, however, Butt and
Raymond's *own* narrative of "horizontal" (counterbiographies) and
"vertical" (multiple drafts) methods of validity-checking demonstrates
again an uneasiness with respect to the fictive nature of the autobiographical undertaking, and displays a hesitancy over the efficacy of
the group processes that they have offered as a collaborative solution
to the problem of validity.

As a result of this hesitancy, they are unwilling to rely entirely on
the intersubjective checks that the collaborative process makes potentially available, and in fact go further. "We ourselves have acted

as participant-observers in our autobiographer-co-researchers' class-rooms and been impressed by the face validity of their accounts, the congruence between the story and our observation" (1989, p. 414). It would seem here that while the collaborative check may well have proved a necessary condition for acceptance by the researchers as to the validity of the autobiographical accounts, it certainly did not prove to be a sufficient condition. Thus when researchers begin from the premise that what they are really after is a congruence between an autobiographical narrative and the so-called "real" events which that narrative points to, then it can lead, as here, to placing the re-searchers in an awkward position. On the one hand, Butt and Ray-mond quite rightly go to great lengths, as have Abbs and Grumet, to ensure that the requisite feelings of trust are built up among the group and in the instructors; on the other hand, the researchers' de-sire to sit in on the teachers' classrooms in order to check out whether the teachers were telling the truth about themselves and their prac-tices provides a broad hint that they may be ambivalent about the status of their own narratives of the teachers' classrooms *as fictional constructions themselves.* This situation, as we will see below, calls for the selection and application of interpretive procedures, procedures over which they show perhaps an exaggerated sense of delicacy. One is therefore driven to question an approach in which the researchers' own narrative constructions and interpretations seem not to be in-cluded as part of the data.

In fairness, Butt and Raymond are aware of the need to adopt some kind of critical framework or interpretive lens by means of which the teachers' autobiographical narratives may be deepened and made more meaningful. However, although they are willing to acknowledge the potential usefulness in applying, for example, psy-choanalytic, feminist, or Marxist frames, as well as the possibility of collaborative interpretations of stories, they have "deliberately cho-sen to do neither" (p. 415). What they would wish is for teachers to "invent their own frameworks" (p. 415), leaving the exploration of alternative frameworks for later. In this instance the authors tantalize at the exact moment when we wish to know more precisely what these self-invented interpretive frameworks are if in fact not some version of psychoanalytic, feminist, or Marxist frames themselves. It is unlikely that because the instructor draws back from suggesting the application of some interpretive approach as a sign of delicacy or the democratic impulse, teachers (or anyone) will be able to bring to birth ab ovo some method of interpretation that is peculiar to them. Rather than enjoin them to invent their own frameworks, perhaps it might be more useful to have them apply whatever frameworks seem comfortable, or that they are familiar with, or to consider responding to their narratives as they might imagine an ideal reader might respond. In their conclusion, however, Butt and Raymond state that it is not in the end the way "that teachers see their own knowledge" that ultimately counts, but the fact that they "think and behave *as if it were true*" (p. 416, emphasis in original). In other words, it is important that teachers come to believe in their own fictions about themselves while making and interpreting these fictions guided by the compelling transparency between word and action, between language and referent, between the shadow and the substance.

In spite, however, of the problems associated with this particular expression of Butt and Raymond's justification for employing autobiographical inquiry as a research method, other works of theirs (1987; Butt, Raymond, & Yamagishi, 1988) that deal in great detail with the autobiographical accounts of specific teachers do seem to result in capturing intriguing phenomenological portraits of those teachers, as well as accounting for the nature of the teachers' own personal practical knowledge. In other words, like both Abbs's and Grumet's preservice students, Butt and Raymond's experienced teachers also discover more about themselves and their situations and how they have evolved as individuals. By taking a strategic view of the circumstances, then, we might say in this instance that the intuitive appeal of autobiography is justified by its results rather than by the sophistication or theoretical acumen that has gone into providing the warrants for its use. What our application of the discoveries made by turning to literary theory has accomplished is not only to have indicated the existence of some theoretical or methodological discrepancies, but has also suggested further possibilities for making existing practices more powerful.

Yet at the same time as we might wish to applaud in Butt and Raymond's work the recognition that a concern for the social nature of any autobiographical undertaking always underscores its use, we might also wish to question whether the inductive aim of generalization from specific cases is not in the long run a chimerical undertaking, and in fact may lead to the very demystification of the special knowledge it is claimed teachers possess and that provides the reason for undertaking the research in the first place. Consequently, it is precisely here that the aims of science and autobiography may be said to contradict each other in that the former aims at the articulation of general laws in order to predict and control the occurrence of phenomena, while autobiography celebrates the freestanding individual consciousness and promotes the writing of autobiography as a *defense* against all of the forces that make for conformity and prediction. The justification for an existential approach to education rests squarely on the fact of subjectivity-in-process, that is, that we are always capable of changing ourselves and the manner of representing ourselves through acts that are freely chosen in order for us to stand out from surroundings that are themselves constantly changing. There is, therefore, no one essential self that informs all that we are and do, but rather a plurality of selves that we can not only discover, create, and deploy in autobiographical acts of writing, but that we can also construct and reconstruct as part of the endless process of becoming.

CONCLUSION

These international perspectives on the arguments and practices put forward for justifying the restructuring of teacher education along autobiographical lines have allowed us to examine both critically and sympathetically a highly contested and important area of concern for education as a whole. There is little doubt that, as all of its proponents allow, such an undertaking is controversial; they would also allow that the extent of the controversy is closely related to some basic lack of appreciation on the part of institutions for the changing status of knowledge within even the most rigorous disciplines such as physics and mathematics. And, as Stodolsky (1988) has pointed out in her book on the state of mathematics teaching in the schools, the cutting-edge discoveries in mathematics of a Kurt Gödel have neither filtered through to inform the approach to mathematics education of teacher training institutions, nor have they made any impact on the day-to-day teaching of mathematics in the schools. There is a limited sense in which the same can be said for the training of language education teachers, although within language education, as we saw in the previous chapter, there exists an alternative and powerful paradigm associated with the work of Britton, Graves, and Smith that travels under the name of whole language as part of what Willinsky (1987, 1990b) has christened the New Literacy. Therefore, while new conceptions of knowledge have not entirely failed to find a home in teacher education, they are still inadequately represented and seem unlikely to act as anything more than a countervailing force, at least for the time being.

Clearly, then, to advocate that the entire preservice year be based on autobiography may be to ask too much of instructors bent on following the consequences or logic of this new epistemology. In fact, Abbs himself recommends that only the first term be spent building up what one might call this autobiographical base; the other two terms are spent in more traditional fashion with introductions to some of the skills and techniques traditionally associated with teacher preparation years, but always with the trainee's recursive response to themselves, their students, and their schools as a continuing locus of concern (Abbs, 1976, pp. 133–138). What the general feeling of these educators seems to be is at once as simple and as complex as the ancient Socratic injunction: One cannot teach others until one "knows oneself" more fully. Autobiography, it is argued, as the vehicle that comes closest to fulfilling this urge toward self-knowledge, not only stands poised to reveal the hidden sources of one's attitude toward one's educational experience, but actually demonstrates the validity of a constructivist approach to knowledge and the workings of a subject-in-process. In this respect, to exhibit a concern for autobiography problematizes many of the abstractions that are said to characterize objective knowledge and, as we have seen throughout, supports the contention of a philosopher like Polanyi (1962) for seeing knowledge as personal and tacit.

Either way, it is clear that whatever portion of time instructors choose to spend on autobiography as a process or a product is, according to the testimony of a majority of undergraduate or graduate students who have participated in such programs, time well and profitably spent. While this chapter has taken pains to explore some aspects of turning toward autobiography that indicate the often severe nature of the demands it makes on both students and instructors alike, I have also tried to counterbalance this with an awareness of the genuine expressions of joy and discovery that often form an integral part of the autobiographical method.

And yet as we will see in the next chapter, Grumet and her colleague William Pinar have advanced a view of autobiography as curriculum theory that not only builds upon the existential and phenomenological foundations covered briefly here, but that finds a further source of warrants in psychoanalysis, an amalgam that has been responsible for the promotion of autobiography as a method of reconceptualizing curriculum studies. Our penultimate chapter on curriculum studies will demonstrate, as has this chapter on teacher education, that wherever autobiography goes, controversy is sure to follow.

6 *Currere* and Reconceptualism: Autobiography as Curriculum Theory

. . . the journey inward becomes an ongoing process that leads out-ward to a more complete understanding of the human condition. Self-understanding is not merely a reflection on what we are but what we are in relation to the world. Self-understanding comes to us via our unique perceptions of the world which are inherent upon our individ-ual abilities as well as on our sociocultural histories.

Florence Krall, 1988

Among the many images or characterizations of curriculum that pres-ently constitute the field of curriculum studies, Schubert (1986) iden-tifies curriculum as *currere* as "one of the most recent positions to emerge on the curriculum horizon" (p. 33). Advocates of this posi-tion, rather than interpreting curriculum etymologically and nomi-nally as a course to be run, choose instead to emphasize the root infi-nitive in order to stress the activity of running, to privilege the individual's own capacity "to reconceptualize his or her autobiogra-phy" (Schubert, 1986, p. 33). There is little doubt in this instance, however, that despite the intellectual superstructure of European phi-losophies invoked by advocates of *currere* to support their position, philosophies that will be examined shortly, John Dewey's idea of cur-riculum as experience stands closest to encapsulating many of *cur-rere*'s broader educational objectives. Dewey's idea that the curricu-lum should not be composed of activities that set predetermined ends or learning outcomes leaves the way clear to conceive of it as a contin-uous process of construction and reconstruction, of active reflection

119

on one's own experience in the service of self-realization (Blewett, 1960; Dewey, 1938, 1960, 1980; Graham, 1989).

In this manner the curriculum can be seen to evolve, since with its focus on the learner (and here we are reminded that a key reconceptualist belief is that the curriculum "is the collective story we tell our children about our past, our present and our future" [Grumet, 1981, p. 115]), it acknowledges the student's search for meaning as an interactive and reflective process undertaken in a social milieu. It is further argued that autobiography as writing the self, as a method of reflecting on and grounding the self in lived experience, comes closest to hand as the prime candidate to accomplish such a task of reconceptualization.

But if Schubert is confident in one way that *currere* is a position to which some workers in curriculum would subscribe, in another way he is just as certain that many others would object strenuously to such a conception. Indeed, he likens the curriculum field itself to the parable of the blind men and the elephant in which each touches a different part of the animal and infers an image of the whole from that. With this caveat in mind, therefore, I want to review *currere*'s progress by an analysis and critique of its original formulation, by situating its emergence historically within curriculum studies, and by examining the kinds of criticisms and objections that persist in dogging its trail. If Pinar (1988) can confidently state that the curriculum field has indeed been reconceptualized, it has been so only to the extent that we are willing to recognize that "it takes some years for everyone, depending on his or her location, to see this" (p. 3). And further, if Pinar is correct in his observation that elementary and secondary schools must become the sites of a "second wave" (1988, p. 13) whereby reconceptualist thought and practice can be filtered into the consciousness of teachers and hence affect the world of practice, then it is imperative that some broad reevaluation of *currere* be advanced that will refresh our understanding and engage us further in critical dialogue. To this end, I will work on a wide front in order to sketch out briefly those aspects of reconceptualization incorporated in both Pinar's and Grumet's notions of autobiographical method. Then will follow a more detailed consideration of the intellectual sources of the method in continental philosophy, as well as an explanation of some of Pinar and Grumet's stated hopes for *currere* as curriculum theory. Finally, some residual problems that have arisen since the method was first formulated, as well as some recent thinking on the topic, will occupy our attention as *currere*'s present status is challenged and discussed.

RETELLING EDUCATIONAL EXPERIENCE:
THE REUSEABLE PAST

If Pinar's edited volume *Curriculum Theorizing: The Reconceptualists* (1975) can fairly be said to have fired a broadside against more traditional conceptions of curriculum, particularly those associated with the "Tyler rationale" (1949) as well as the work of the so-called conceptual-empiricists (Schubert's social behaviorists), who use empirical methods to predict and control curricular phenomena, then Pinar's own four contributions in that volume (Pinar, 1975a, 1975b, 1975c, 1975d) were individual bullets from the sniper's rifle of a guerrilla band of self-styled "reconceptualists." In one of these essays Pinar (1975c) took direct aim not only at Tyler but also at Huebner (1975), a figure sympathetic to reconceptualism, who in the same volume insisted that the task of the curriculum theorist was "to articulate the uses of language within the curricular domain, and to identify the various modes of language used" (pp. 256–257).

By shifting the focus of attention away from a technical rationale, with its concentration on design and objectives, toward dwelling on the nature of one's inner experience, Pinar (1975c) offered *currere*—"the investigation of the nature of the individual experience of the public: of artifacts, actors, operations, of the educational journey or pilgrimage" (p. 400)—as a knowledge-producing method of inquiry appropriate for the study of educational experience. As we will shortly discover in more detail, by calling upon the traditions of existentialism, phenomenology, and psychoanalysis, Pinar hoped to be able to analyze educational experience, to reconstruct curriculum materials in terms of the individual's own consciousness. Pinar (1975c) echoed with approval in another essay Maxine Greene's sentiments that reconstructing an artifact (here a narrative of educational experience) in terms of one's own consciousness was "to allow it presence within me, uncritically, to observe it and how it 'fits,' if it is the next 'piece' in the developing intellectual gestalt, to 'test it' against memories of past experience" (p. 408).

And it is in the essay entitled "The Analysis of Educational Experience" that Pinar (1975b) provides the outline of an autobiographical method that is directed at illuminating how our "domain assumptions" (p. 388) form a part of the larger inner world that is equivalent for Pinar to Husserl's *lebenswelt*. Although Pinar wants to argue that this reconstructing of experience has similarities with Dewey's project except that it has a different end, namely, the slow transcendence of self from circumstances rather than the Deweyan notion of adapting self to circumstances, in practice it wholly supports, under certain provisos, an aesthetic approach to self-realization, one whose consequences are compatible with the kinds of knowledge claims people have traditionally turned to autobiography to supply. In sum, Pinar's (1975b) early characterization of autobiographical method involves three steps:

> . . . first to render one's educational experience . . . into words, using the associative form of minding. The second is to use one's critical faculties to understand what principles and patterns have been operative in one's educational life, hence achieving a more profound understanding of one's educational experience, as well as illuminating parts of the inner world and deepening one's self-understanding generally. The third task is to analyze other's experience to reveal what I call basic educational structures or processes that cross biographical lines. (p. 389)

It is crucial to take note that Pinar's (1975b) conception of the self does not involve the traditional id-ego-superego triad of Freudian psychology, but rather involves Husserl's idea of a transcendental ego, a structure that "remains continuous over time and permits observation of lower-level psychic workings" (p. 390). In effect, the method would work like a Rorschach inkblot test, drawing out by means of association unconscious material regarding the nature of the individual's educational experience. Although Pinar is alive to several immediate objections to the method, objections centered mainly around the ethical constraints that may have to accompany its use as an instrument of research, as well as the inevitable problems of transference (on both of which more later), he maintains that this "translation of private *lebenswelt* into public language" (p. 391) will assist in healing the breach between much educational research and its perceived separation from the actual experiences of teachers and students in educational settings. Likewise, Pinar wastes no time in asserting that in this necessarily slow and long-term effort can be discovered possibilities for transcendence, a process that he would hold involves a potent sense of becoming through excavating and bringing to light that which has been buried by many years of schooling and social conditioning. In his later, more elaborate formulation of *currere* as a regressive-progressive-analytical-synthetical method, Pinar (1976c) states that his method "is the self conscious conceptualization of the temporal . . . [undertaken] to explore the complex relation between the temporal and the conceptual. In doing so we disclose their relation to the Self in its evolution and education" (p. 51).

For Pinar's colleague Grumet the relationship of autobiography to the reconceptualization of curriculum is also discovered in the reflexive project implied by the very nature of the autobiographical urge toward retelling episodes from our life stories. However, the ultimate significance of the episodes that emerge from this narrative undertaking is not found in their existence "as pieces of literature, as ends in themselves" (Grumet, 1976c, p. 116), but rather "as precipitates of a developmental process in which the telling and reading and revising" (p. 116) are of the utmost importance. Although it is clear that some inchoate principle of selection is involved in foregrounding some experiences and in excluding others, nevertheless Grumet claims that these abstractions themselves can become the subject of inquiry. And as several commentators have noted in discussing the position of autobiography in literary theory (Benstock, 1988; Eakin, 1985; Egan, 1984; Friedman, 1988; Smith, 1987), these texts and the information selected for inspection can work in the service of predicting future behavior and courses of action. Consequently, from this entirely fictional operation Grumet argues that curriculum is reconceptualized in two ways.

First, as with Pinar's free-associative method, experiences are reclaimed through a reflective process that begins by allowing the mind to wander, and continues by providing rich details and descriptions in order to situate the narrative, to place it in the specifics of a thoroughly evoked context. Grumet (1976a, p. 40) appeals in this connection to Merleau-Ponty's notion of "pre-predicative experience" in order to connect the images thus evoked to the subject who underwent the experience. It is only in the "freshness and immediacy" (p. 39) of our narratives of lived experience that the curriculum can be reconceptualized, since the narratives reclaim entire areas of experience from the associations that represent for the individual the feeling-tone of the experience itself.

Second, as these narratives are analyzed, "interests and biases" (p. 41) that are often hidden in the normal course of living stand revealed for inspection. Autobiography as text, as fiction, as an aesthetic artifact that represents the way in which we have chosen to order and interpret our experience, is primed to reveal to us the nature and extent of our freedom. In this manner educational experience is reordered into "a usable past [and] into a usable present" (p. 41) whose purpose is contained in the existential aim of promoting a sense of personal responsibility for our actions. However, the organicism implied in this construction of narrative, in the reconstruction and patterning of experience to provide an appearance of wholeness, is not undertaken to paper over the cracks in our view of the world but rather to "reach back through our experience to the preconceptual encounter that is the foundation of our judgments" (p. 41), a purpose that transcends the escape afforded by the consolation and comfort of aesthetic representation alone.

Even from this truncated exposition of autobiographical method we not only can move some way toward situating *currere* within the field of curriculum studies in general, but also can examine how the initial criticism leveled at *currere* from adherents to other, more dominant curricular paradigms created various kinds of struggle and tension in the field. This struggle is by no means over, in spite of Pinar's claims to the contrary and the move by Schubert and others (McNeil, 1985; Ornstein & Hunkins, 1988) to legitimate the reconceptualist paradigm in their synoptic textbooks of the field itself. It is clear that the kind of hornet's nest *currere* stirred up in the field involved more than an argument over the adequacy of which conceptual lenses one wore to examine curricular phenomena, but in fact addressed a series of sensitive issues that struck at the heart of professional reputations, at political and social ideologies, at aspirations for education, and indeed at permutations of all three.

If we employ for the sake of convenience Schubert's (1986) designation that there exist within the curriculum field three competing paradigms—the *empirical/analytic* represented by Ralph Tyler, the *hermeneutic* represented by Joseph Schwab (although Schubert is rightly unhappy about applying this to Schwab's particular version of "the practical"), and the *critical* represented by William Pinar—then in the terms given currency by the German philosopher Jurgen Habermas (1971), the "interest" served by each paradigm would be, consecutively, the *technical,* the *practical,* and the *emancipatory.* There is little space here to recapitulate in any detail Habermas's theory of knowledge and its cultural implications; suffice it to say that the empirical/analytic orientation is interested in control and certainty, in social reality as it is, and contains a theory of knowledge as value-free and objective. Hermeneutic inquiry serves the practical interest and understands reality as intersubjectively constituted, emphasizes communicative interaction, and views knowledge as the creation of human beings. Finally, the critical paradigm serves an emancipatory interest that concentrates on the uses and abuses of power, encourages a sensitivity to false consciousness, and seeks to expose whatever is oppressive and dominating (see Geuss, 1981, pp. 45–54).

Under this particular schema, *currere* and much reconceptualist thinking in general can be clearly subsumed, with differences in emphasis, within both hermeneutic and critical paradigms, since their concentration on the autobiographical act and other discoveries within the humanities largely presupposes an interest in self-discovery, in relations with others, and in the possibilities for personal change, healing, and transformation. Broadly speaking, then, when Pinar, Grumet, and other reconceptualists challenge present ways of thinking and talking about schooling and its effects on individuals, they are saying at the same time that in a curriculum driven by product-oriented methodologies and by technologies of knowledge and evaluation that are firmly in the grasp of textbook publishers and bureaucratic administrators, many of the ethical and aesthetic dimensions of education are being willfully ignored or forgotten.

Perhaps more disturbing for an influential critic and curriculum worker like Jackson (1981) than the move away from previous reliance on the empirical methods of mainstream social science was the privileging of European traditions of thought, sources that were not only politically left of center but that were, it was claimed by reconceptualists, more fruitful for thinking about educational events than the native American traditions that had to that point dominated the scene. In addition, and as a corollary to this move, Jackson noted a concomitant change in the relationship between those who study and write about curriculum (academics) and those who work in schools (teachers). In practice this works out to two separate positions, one calling for a closer relationship as in the work of Butt and Raymond (1987), and the other calling for a more distant relationship as in the estimation of some major reconceptualist thinkers. This latter position is justified on the basis that only by maintaining a critical perspective with respect to curricular matters can education and the curriculum be viewed outside of narrow and officially sanctioned conceptions of schooling.

Whatever the merits of this altered relationship, Jackson reserves most of his own critical remarks for the use made by reconceptualists of specifically European intellectual traditions. Although applauding the fact that reconceptualist thinking is "refreshing" and "better written" (1981, p. 379) on the whole than most educational criticism, he is annoyed "by too many signs of in-groupiness and too many lapses into a sophomoric profundity, characterized by half-baked thoughts and a vulgar display of partially digested knowledge" (p. 379), where words like *lebenswelt* and *weltanschauung* are "plopped like German dumplings into the thin broth of Anglo-Saxon prose in the hope, I suppose, of thickening it" (p. 379). Likewise, the Tanners (1981) argue that not only does reconceptualism fail to conform to criteria that would qualify it in any way as a movement, but that Pinar's work itself illegitimately employs Habermas's categories, rejects research of the conceptual-empirical model of the social sciences, and instead proposes the "mystical alchemy" (p. 389), where the move toward autobiographical reflection and contemplation can somehow be made "through a transcendental-existential levitation" (p. 389) to ensure the emancipatory interest in the way designated by Habermas himself.

As indicated earlier, it is these kinds of criticisms, regardless of their often ad hominem quality, that have been leveled at Pinar and his work with *currere*. Pinar's paper, "A Reply to My Critics" (1981), is of interest in this respect, for two major assertions are made by Pinar that are of direct concern for the curriculum field and for the position of autobiography within it. These assertions are: (1) that reconceptualization is not a movement comprised of leaders and adherents, but a term used to describe "a fundamental shift—a paradigm shift— in the orders of research conducted by diverse curricularists" (p. 394); and (2) that "this method [*currere*] and the view of curriculum embedded in it, are developed to considerable theoretical maturity in *Toward a Poor Curriculum*" (p. 395). It is Pinar's claim that had the Tanners studied more carefully this latter work (coauthored with Grumet), they would not have tried to reduce his work to "warmed-over sixties critique" (p. 395). Both of Pinar's propositions were issued in the form of a challenge, yet to this point neither has been taken up in a systematic way by Pinar's critics. The first assertion, that reconceptualism represents a paradigm shift, has, however, been addressed by Brown (1988) and will occupy us presently. An examination of the second assertion remains to be accomplished, and it is a move toward creating the initial conditions for this task that will be undertaken in the following section.

CHANGING THE FIELD:
AN INTELLECTUAL FRAMEWORK FOR *CURRERE*

In 1981, Pinar enlisted the assistance of T. M. Brown, a historian of science at the University of Rochester, to ascertain whether reconceptualization was indeed a paradigm shift under the terms made popular by Thomas Kuhn (1970). Pinar provided Brown with a range of materials, including the work of Jackson, the Tanners, and himself, to which Brown responded by producing a coolly reasoned assessment of the appropriateness of applying the idea of reconceptualization to the field of curriculum. It is unnecessary to rehearse again as Brown does the familiar features involved in a Kuhnian paradigm shift within a scientific discipline; what is of interest is the kinds of tentative conclusions Brown thought it pertinent to draw with respect to judging the apparent crisis in the quasi-scientific or nonscientific field of curriculum.

Brown's (1988) conclusion, based on his examination of Jackson's critique of Pinar and reconceptualization, is that "a first approximation" (p. 26) to a paradigm shift seems to be under way. However, he cites the Tanners' complaints as evidence that any application of Kuhn's ideas to a field other than science "must be done carefully and cautiously" (p. 27). Therefore, if we should expect that in a field such as curriculum claims for a paradigm shift ought to be advanced with the appropriate degree of caution, what kind of evidence would begin to tip the scales in favor of agreeing that a shift has occurred? True to his Kuhnian training, Brown advocates a sociological study of the curriculum field in order to find out not only who curricularists are, but also to discover "what institutional positions they occupy, [and] what degree of training in what disciplines they have received" (p. 28). This kind of information would provide a more thorough understanding of the academic preparation of workers in curriculum and hence the different "worldviews" brought to its study, as well as monitor the generational aspects of the field since, as Kuhn believes, new paradigms can arise when older members of the field die off to leave the field clear for other views to take over. In this instance it would appear that the field did pass through a crisis (the 1960s) where a new generation was born whose influence is only now being felt as that generation reaches maturity, gains a foothold in institutions, and begins to challenge the received wisdom and traditional points of view.

Interestingly for what is to follow, Brown takes up Jackson's criticism that reconceptualists in general subscribe to the notion that they should sever their ties with practitioners in order to develop a pure theory of curriculum. Brown offers two observations in support of Jackson's position. First, it is too early to develop pure theory in the curriculum field, since even Newton had to rely on his predecessors before he could develop his theory of mechanics as he did. For curricularists, "Mere wishing and straining won't make it so; the time has to be ripe for a Newton to appear" (p. 29). Second, even if something like the *Principia* already exists in the field, "very few of the older generation are likely to be persuaded until it proves capable of addressing more successfully than its competitors the ongoing problems in the field" (p. 29). However, by concentrating on satisfying the demands imposed by the older generation, reconceptualism may be shouldering an unnecessary burden. Hence the dilemma: If reconceptualism ignores the older problems, it too "risks being ignored" (p. 29); if it takes up these problems it risks cutting itself off from new sources of creativity and thinking. Therefore, if the reconceptualists want to claim that there has indeed been a paradigm shift rather than, as Brown (1988) puts it, "a proliferation of schools" (p. 28), then he also wonders what kind of harm would accrue if the new curricularists really did engage with the so-called anomalies of the older established conceptual-empirical research program.

While Brown's conclusions are properly tempered and cautious, and while there may not yet have appeared a Newton who will irrevocably alter our thinking on curriculum, serious questions remain regarding the capacity of reconceptualism to demonstrate any abiding concern or interest in perennial issues such as curriculum change and implementation. Pinar may be correct in claiming that there is a "significant reduction in the field's resistance to the Reconceptualists" (1988b, p. 1); but they have yet to move in any satisfactory way beyond acting as a ginger group or the self-appointed voice of conscience in a field they claim is ruled by technical rationality and an instrumentalist intention. However, even to succeed in this limited way is to perform a great service to the field. Indeed, Posner (1988) may come closer to the mark when he writes that the function of the critical perspective in the field of curriculum "raises our consciousness regarding the assumptions underlying our work in curriculum. By giving us ground to stand on outside the dominant approach, it has enabled us to examine critically the technical production perspective, to identify its blind spots, and to understand its political and social implications" (p. 94).

In other words, the work of Beauchamp, Tyler, Taba, the Tanners, and Schwab still continues to represent the dominant thinking on how to think about or develop a curriculum, thinking that correctly draws attention to the procedures and concepts involved in attempting to plan a curriculum along rational lines. However, reconceptualist thought seems largely uninterested in, and deeply disagrees with, these procedural models, preferring instead to attack them from ideological and political points of view. Nevertheless, Posner may again come closest when he argues that both perspectives are required by any model of curriculum that seeks comprehensive status. Not only technique is required, but also what Posner calls "a curriculum conscience" (1988, p. 94), since a curriculum planned without the former "is incompetent," and without the latter "is ungrounded" (p. 94). Reconceptualist thinking is valuable, even necessary, to the extent that it makes us aware of the often hidden implications of a particular technical model, and may in addition help answer Walker and Soltis's (1986) curriculum dilemma: "How to proceed when aims and priorities are unstable and shifting?" (p. 76).

In spite of all this, however, there still exist residual doubts regarding the existence of a paradigm shift in the terms Pinar proposes. It would be irresponsible speculation to guess why Pinar insists on mounting a campaign for reconceptualism as a paradigm shift, but clearly there is a real sense in which he might be said to protest too much. What must be inspected in the meantime, however, is the idea that if reconceptualization more accurately describes the work of a small and heterogeneous collection of individuals from different intellectual backgrounds who share certain loosely defined aims, then a majority of those would subscribe to the governing principle "of finding ways of coming to know oneself as organically embedded in culture and history and needing to rely more on experience" (Schubert, 1986, p. 178). It is here that autobiography enters the picture in the form of *currere*, and it is with revealing the framework for *currere* as curriculum theory that Pinar and Grumet are concerned in *Toward a Poor Curriculum* (1976). If not precisely a *Principia*, the book's exploration of the existential, phenomenological, and psychoanalytic bases for *currere* is an intellectual tour de force and must on all accounts be reckoned with. Only then will we be in a position to judge it more fairly and to gauge the possible extent of its continued status as a seminal document in the field of curriculum.

Existential and Phenomenological Foundations

For Grumet (1976a), "the essential and enduring concern" (p. 32) of her kind of curriculum theorist is with metatheory. By continually questioning the presuppositions of the conceptual lenses or metaphors elected to scrutinize educational experience, the aim of curricularists is to contain the experience without reducing it, "to analyze it without atomizing it" (p. 32). To speak of education, then, is to speak not only of one's experience in the world, but to move beyond the merely descriptive toward a definition that "will diminish the discrepancy between public performance and private experience" (p. 34). In other words, for an experience to be educational, as with Dewey, it must be a blend of objectivity and subjectivity, an encounter that changes and extends its immediate significance even as it subtly alters and informs the individual's psyche itself. Grumet wants to view education in these terms as "a person's dialogue with the world of experience" (p. 34), a definition that allows her to argue for finding a theory-base for autobiography in phenomenology, where knowledge of the world requires "knowledge of self-as-knower-of-the-world" (p. 35), and in existentialism, which emphasizes the dialectical nature of the relationship of individuals to their situations. Within the phenomenological tradition, in particular within the work of Husserl, whose central insistence on the *epoché* implied the paradox that only by distancing ourselves from our experience could we begin to come closer to it, Grumet finds a provocative way of conceptualizing the dialectical relationship between humanity and the world.

However, *currere* scales down these somewhat grandiose speculations to the level of the individual in order to make the claim that only by taking into account the situated particularity of the individual can the tendencies within a curriculum designed in discrete and fragmented units be effectively overcome. What *currere* promises, then, as the cornerstone of a reconceptualized curriculum, is nothing less than "the safe return of my own voice" (p. 37). Autobiography, as an intentional act of consciousness, ensures that by bracketing off, remembering, and describing the objects of consciousness, the knowledge so gained would be grounded in the lived experience of the individual. Grumet (1976a) suggests, after Merleau-Ponty, that if the bracketing provided by the *epoché* can "slacken the intentional threads which attach us to the world" (p. 41), then Pinar's *currere*, especially those aspects of it where we take on "the role of the artist and the epistemological posture of the phenomenologist" (p. 53) in order to gain access to the level of our preconceptual encounters, promises to put our "essences back into existence" (p. 41). *Currere* in its employment of the *epoché* is designed to cleanse our cognitive lenses so that through the analysis of educational experience we can make contact with the essential forms of our being.

In addition, Grumet's understanding of the existentialist bases of *currere* causes her to stress the rootedness of all human action in a lived context or situation. If one of the basic tenets of existentialism is that we are condemned to be free, in other words, that we can surpass the facticity of our lives through our free choices, then our self-knowledge develops not primarily by means of introspection, but in the dialectic interplay involved when an embodied subject acts in the world (Grumet, 1987). In this way *currere* attempts to reconcile the paradox of phenomenology, where to distance oneself is to come closer, with the tensions in existentialism between means and ends, of living always situated in the world and yet assuming responsibility for our actions in it.

Psychoanalytic Foundations

The chapter in *Toward a Poor Curriculum* in which Grumet examines *currere's* relationship to psychoanalysis also marks the point at which much of the metatheoretical exposition is brought to earth, as it were, by becoming more explicit over what part she would see *currere* play in our schools and colleges. As she states, she is "less interested in autobiography as a record of a student's passage through schooling . . . than as a source of energy and direction for the journey" (Grumet, 1976c, p. 111). By initially drawing on Olney's distinction in *Metaphors of Self* (1972) between the autobiography of the single metaphor that describes a life already completed, and the autobiography of the double metaphor in which "the life story is identical with the life process that created it and is indeed an extension of that process" (Grumet, 1976c, pp. 111–112), Grumet wants to establish the educational application of *currere* as following the path of the double metaphor. As "a dynamic method of self renewal" (p. 112), autobiography as practiced in *currere* employs the double metaphor approach, a method that holds that "to describe one's own developmental process is to generate it as well" (p. 112). Grumet begins in this manner because she wishes to claim that psychoanalysis itself operates on the double metaphor principle as a discipline that combines "the specificity and symbolic ambiguity of literature with the generalities and recurring patterns of the social sciences" (p. 112). The problem involved in bringing *currere* into the classroom is the problem exemplified in the project of psychoanalysis itself: how to account for the polarities of "consciousness and the unconscious, individuality and humanity" (p. 112). *Currere*, then, is conceptualized as a form of ego psychology that examines and interprets experience for its manifest and latent meaning "as well as the political implications of reflection and interpretation" (p. 113). In other words, *currere* is a method for giving voice to private experience within a public setting and speaks to the developing structures of a student's personality as it interacts with social and institutional forms and structures.

In addition, while Grumet (1976c) insists that the essence of *cur-*

rere is to be found in the assertion "that *new structures evolve in the process of naming old ones*" (p. 115, emphasis in original), she also holds fast to the notion that *currere* "is not a form of therapy designed to treat symptoms" (p. 115). It cannot claim in this instance that, like psychoanalysis, self-reflection can liberate the individual from the grip of unconscious impulses, but must settle on the less spectacular, and perhaps no less contentious, claim, "that by bringing the structures of experience to awareness, one enhances his ability to direct the process of his own development" (p. 115). Although we will have more to say below in connection with this and other aspects of *currere* as it relates to Pinar's hopes for a second wave of reconceptualist thought permeating the schools, it is necessary here to follow Grumet's argument to its conclusion.

One of the mainstays of *currere*'s method is that it asks students the question, "what does this mean to you?" (p. 116). In order to focus what significance the students' educational experience has been for them, the writing of autobiography provides a response to that question. These narratives are then translated or interpreted in a dialogue between a student and herself or with the instructor. This hermeneutic project transforms lived experience into language in order to intensify the student's experience, and hence it encourages students to give voice to their own meanings. In addition, Grumet (1976b) wants to use autobiography with teachers in order that they will become "conscious of their fictions so they will not be ruled by their myths" (p. 74), and with students to make them conscious of their constitutive metaphors. By the process of self-objectification, the student can begin to examine the relations between the ego and all those items best described as nonego, from fantasies and wishes to the structure and demands of the academic disciplines undergone in schools.

Similarly, although *currere*'s commitment to the growth of the student means in practice that it is committed to unbuckling what psychoanalyst Wilhelm Reich called our "character armor," Grumet is anxious to reassure educators and society at large (who, she claims, fear all expressions of internal experience) that *currere* is not about to "unleash a libidinous behemoth to topple cognitive structure, public schooling and Western civilization with its untamed instinctual energies" (1976c, p. 122), but that, mindful of Freud's injunction "where Id was there shall Ego be," it will proceed more prosaically "to help students recover their own intentionality and find there the energy for their academic work as well as the links that connect that [sic] it to the concerns and events of their daily experience" (p. 123). Grumet is aware that this pursuit of self-knowledge is neither new nor radical; it is in fact a direct legacy from at least Socratic times, fortified with a healthy dose of Romanticism (Willinsky, 1990a). What is ironic, she claims, is that we have succeeded in producing a culture that "estranges us from ourselves" (p. 126) and that has preserved "the products of its self-consciousness in museums and libraries" (p. 126). Schools have then been content to concentrate on these objects rather than on the "subjective processes" (p. 126) that brought them into being. A genuinely dialectical pedagogy would attempt to restore a deeply felt sense of self, and in this case would fulfill the distinguishing qualities of both literature and psychoanalysis, namely, that they "subvert the official text of the culture" (p. 127).

But if we would want to object that the subversive fruits of self-consciousness and self-knowledge not only might get tempered and normalized by the adjustment mythology that rules over the mentality of many teachers, and also that Grumet seems to be talking here of fairly sophisticated students in the upper grades of high school, she is quick to point out that *currere* has an integral part to play even in elementary school. In this site, *currere* would function "to reinforce the dialectical relationship of the family and the school" (p. 128). By attending to the very young child's experience of the curriculum (presumably in the autobiographical form of journals and other expressive writing, although this is never made clear), *currere* repeats "the maternal and paternal principles" (p. 128). That is, *currere* repeats "the patterns of ego development initiated in the infant's early object relations" (p. 128). The goal here is not adversarial; *currere* would not drive a wedge between the school, the child, and the family, but rather it would "establish sufficient distance so that the child will not be subsumed by the school" (p. 128). Here the maternal principle of trust in the mother (and in mother-surrogates like teachers) is reconciled with the paternal principle that what is seen as alien, as a stranger, can be introjected.

Finally, although by no means exhausting the relation Grumet adduces between *currere* and psychoanalysis, the problem of transference rears its head. While Grumet acknowledges that some measure of transference does take place as an instructor responds to the autobiographical narratives (transference takes place in most teaching situations), realizing this may assist in checking its development. Likewise, the educational use of *currere* differs from the emotional intensity of the psychoanalytic relationship by rejecting "the aura of insight" (1976c, p. 139) of the instructor, and by acknowledging that in working with so many groups of students the instructor has neither "the time nor training" (p. 140) to fully participate in the transferences that characterize the full-blown therapist-patient relationship. Further, the instructor can diminish the possibility of her own dispro-portionate influence by engaging other students as co-respondents, and by keeping firmly in mind the idea that *currere* is a developmental process that would see experience "as diffuse and relative but also as intelligible, continuous and self-directed" (p. 140). Autobiography as a provocative blend of fiction, personal metaphor, and myth is under-taken to make students aware that this method of self-representation is less concerned with a wholly accurate rendering of what was the case; rather, it is to be hoped that a student will assume a more relativ-istic stance in order to facilitate reviewing an educational experience as part of his or her life history "without at the same time repudiating it or affirming it" (Grumet, 1976c, p. 135). *Currere* does not wish to alter basic personality structures but instead holds out to students a method of gaining more direct access to the personal meaning of the experience of schooling.

CONCLUSION

As we saw earlier when Schubert's tripartite characterization of the curriculum field was offered as a convenient way of situating recon-ceptualism and *currere*, advocates of the paradigm of critical praxis share to varying degrees a concentration on the ideological ramifica-tions of curriculum. Reconceptualists, in concert with social recon-structionists and critical theorists of the Frankfurt school persuasion, are interested in such pertinent issues as how knowledge is repro-duced in schools (Whitty, 1985), how students, especially those from less privileged backgrounds, resist the impositions of school knowl-edge (Giroux, 1988), and how students and teachers alike can be moved in the direction of more emancipatory teaching and learning practices. On the face of it, a clear understanding of Dewey's work, particularly classic statements like *Democracy and Education*, combined with an appreciation for his role in the social reconstructionist move-ment and its journal *The Social Frontier* (see Bowers, 1969, pp. 48–88), could stand as emblematic of a fully developed program for emanci-pation that combines a method of inquiry with critique and praxis. Grumet (1981), however, would distance the project of *currere* from Dewey's work, and it is in what she has to say to justify this position that a beginning can be made at summing up and clarifying what is at once attractive in autobiographical method for some curricularists of her persuasion, and yet what has proved so forbidding for others who are more convinced by the arguments of Jackson or the Tanners.

According to Grumet (1981), Pinar's autobiographical method of *currere* "was a project of restitution, wresting experience from the anonymity and generalisation that had dominated the social sciences . . . and returning it to the particular persons who lived it" (p. 116). Her own first task was in the nature of a rescue operation: to save "autobiography from its association with the self, the alias that has given subjectivity a bad name" (p. 116). The psychoanalytic foundation of *currere* emphasizes a return to an inspection of the manifest and latent content of our inner experience as expressed in narrative, and to all those items like dreams and fantasies that, as we saw previously, formed part of the nonego, and which contain our visions of possibility for ourselves and society. However, Grumet feels that the surplus repressions of advanced capitalism make it impossible to bring our dreams "into the discourse of daily life" (p. 118), and so we disguise them under a "bourgeois notion of selfhood" (p. 119), a designation that Lasch's (1978) term the "culture of narcissism" captures well. The paradox of this state of false consciousness is that even as we are enjoined to celebrate the self, to cultivate all expressions of a rich subjectivity, we are irrevocably tied to the status quo, a relation in which there are few signs of "the tension and struggle of feeling and form that releases subjectivity" (p. 119). Dewey is criticized here not for grounding subjectivity in the social, which he so evidently did, but for his "conciliatory" (p. 120) approach to the Freudian insight that society is maintained at the price of repression. The scenario painted here by Grumet is the familiar one of the conflict between the liberal notion of adjustment to established forms in society, with the possibilities for transcendence implicated in the radical critique. It is Dewey's confidence that his cherished principles of inquiry would be sufficient to deal with the questions and uncertainties encountered in our daily living that Grumet is determined to resist. Curriculum theory must "rigorously root out optimism" (p. 122) if it is to function as anything more than an ideological support for restrictive liberal (read capitalistic) practices; likewise, progressive education "collapses into the most insidious form of cooptation" (p. 122) unless it is also motivated to challenge our most deeply held ideologies. Finally, "it is suspicion that this autobiographical method cultivates. . . . Suspicion is a response to a solution" (p. 122).

When cast in these terms, it is easier to see the threat that making the personal political would represent for a variety of stakeholders in the curriculum: researchers, professors, superintendents, teachers, and parents whose conceptions of curriculum are more oriented toward improving test scores and in maintaining clear standards of accountability than in shadowy concepts like emancipation. It is small wonder, then, that the charge of warmed-over 1960s critique, a charge that for these educators would bring back memories of commentators like Postman and Weingartner (1969), who conceived of teaching as a subversive activity, has been constantly leveled at the reconceptualist wing of the curriculum field.

And yet if the experience of the 1960s, from Students for a Democratic Society to Kent State, has left its mark on this new generation of curricularists, then this legacy has made them realize that the appeal of autobiography resides less in its Romantic claim to return to us a vision of that which was lost, a vision of the Garden before the Fall (Lifson, 1979), but rather in its psychological and political capacity to mine the sedimented layers of consciousness where repression reigns in order to raise consciousness to a level where the uses and abuses of power in our lives are seen in stark relief. In this sense, then, Pinar's accusations of a generational conflict would seem to ring true: consciousness-raising and political involvement of the sort practiced in the 1960s and early 1970s would appear anathema to previous (and present) generations of scholars weaned on the methods (and often visible successes) of the social sciences. Thus, even if traditionalists could be persuaded to see nothing amiss in insisting that students compose narratives of their educational experience and engage in an undertaking whose outcome may well be feelings of anger and injustice, it is quite another matter to maintain that out of these are likely to emerge concrete proposals for reconstituted curricula that are applicable on a large scale for implementation in every school in the nation. Likewise, it is a far cry from claiming that *currere*, by methodically utilizing the autobiographical impulse, can perform wonders for making increasing numbers of students aware that their lives contain both power and possibility, to claiming that *currere* alone represents the royal road to both the personal and collective search for meaning that is the human side of curriculum.

But even if Pinar (1988b) today can state that ideas like cultural revolution and heightened consciousness are "dated terms that make one wince" (p. 3), there is still little doubt that the consciousness-raising element in autobiography is always and intimately related to its use. Therefore it may be worth pointing out here the distance between, for example, Grumet's (1976c) rhetoric that *currere* will restore to students their "intentionality" and "the energy for academic work"

(p. 123), as well as forge connecting links between school and the outside world (all very bourgeois liberal objectives), and the kind of political consciousness-raising that is the not-so-hidden curriculum of the radical hopes for *currere*. If the practice of *currere* does indeed have a place in our elementary and secondary schools as a means of transcendence rather than as another instrument of ideological oppression wielded by teachers as the unwitting dupes of an all-powerful state apparatus (Althusser, 1971), then there is something understandable about those who would downplay the unpredictable vagaries of the transference phenomenon and other items too "hot" for the untrained teacher to handle. To seek to bracket off only the world of educational experience in one breath, and then to encourage students to forge links and connections with the lived world of experience outside the school in the next, could be interpreted as a shrewd strategic move that recognizes the generally low tolerance level of principals and superintendents for any new pedagogy that is politically dubious. But it could also be interpreted as ultimately ambivalent about its own chances of success as a radical instrument of consciousness, and is content to settle for the weaker and more acceptable compromise of giving students motivation and energy to do their homework and to better themselves by something approaching a pride-in-your-roots movement. All of which is to cast doubt on the feasibility of employing the autobiographical method in the public schools with anything approaching the kind of radical potential claimed for it, particularly when it is conceded in advance that teachers have neither the time nor the training (and certainly not the radical consciousness) to implement it thoroughly.

At the same time, however, it is equally clear that part of the continuing attractiveness of *currere* for an increasing number of educators emanates precisely from the courage with which it seeks to make the silences in our educational experience speak. It is indeed the fortunate adult who can reflect on his or her schooling without some residual sense of conflict, of feelings of inadequacy, or of being excluded. Schooling is, after all, as Dewey reminded us, life itself, not a preparation for life. The texts that the autobiographical method makes available for interpretation, then, are interesting to the extent that what they uncover is the manner in which teachers and students alike have been accomplices and victims of the kinds of oppressive relations fostered in educational institutions. This is the kind of payoff that may result when individuals go to work on their own memories. The relationship with the self is transformed, as well as the thematic or metaphoric elements of the remembered material itself. The hope is that when enough individuals are encouraged and enabled to move in this direction, then changes in the social order will also be precipitated.

Clearly, while both Pinar and Grumet are in accord over the ideal ends of *currere* expressed in both personal and social terms, there do exist some tensions that separate these two thinkers. If Grumet is scathing in her denunciation of Dewey's thinking insofar as it kowtows to the maintenance of the status quo and notions of adjustment, Pinar seems content to rely on a more gradual approach to bringing about the social and educational millennium. On the other hand, it is also clear that of all the figures in education who have concerned themselves in a practical way with autobiography, Pinar and Grumet have by far the most fully developed and sophisticated understanding of its special characteristics and ideal potential. Be that as it may, and irrespective of their own undoubtedly courageous and enlightened practices, autobiography as part of "the politics of personal knowledge" (Grumet, 1987, p. 322), when employed in the service of teachers and researchers, continues to raise serious issues regarding the ethics of the situation. As Grumet knows, every retelling is a form of alienation; it is small wonder, then, that teachers who are requested to reconstruct narratives of experience generally exhibit a wide range of dissimulative behavior. In the same manner that students surveyed by Barnes, Barnes, and Clarke (1984) in Chapter 4 were often unwilling to disclose personal details to a teacher with whom they may not have been on the best of terms, so too Grumet (1987) realizes that telling a story even to a friend is also "a risky business" (p. 321), a fact that makes it doubly uncertain when the recipient is a professor or researcher. In other words, Grumet's open acknowledgment of the political and personal ramifications of narrative work extends our ability to visualize some of the drawbacks, as well as many of the long-term advantages, to autobiographical method.

This analysis has gone some way toward fulfilling the restricted and limited aim of providing points of entry into a key element in an important school of thought within curriculum studies. In general, however, the position of reconceptualism within curriculum studies continues to prove fluid and contested. For now, therefore, Pinar (1988b) may be guilty of overstatement when he claims that reconceptualism, something that "started as an opposition to the mainstream and tradition of the field" (p. 7), has now become the field itself; and further, that in his eagerness to announce the paradigm shift as a fait accompli, he has deliberately sidestepped the important empirical and procedural questions that Brown put forward as the acid test for judging the claims of reconceptualism as a whole. But perhaps it is in the long run asking too much of reconceptualism that it may ever provide the kind of empirical and replicable proof that would satisfy (and convert) more traditionally minded curricularists. Rather, the appeal of reconceptualism and of autobiographical method in particular may continue to reside, like a penchant for existential philosophy, in the willingness to accede to the cultivation of a particular perspective, a psychological readiness to believe in its persuasive force as critique and conscience regardless of the difficulties in its application or in its local successes with teachers and students.

And yet it is extremely likely that, in typical Kuhnian fashion, a new generation of scholars sympathetic to reconceptualist thinking is slowly in the process of coming into its own. If this is so, it may signify that for a significant number of workers in curriculum, reconceptualism still represents one of the best hopes for keeping the human factor alive in education, especially in a time of widespread political retrenchment, a global movement whose impetus at present shows few signs of exhaustion.

7   Beyond Autobiography: Concluding Poststructural Postscript

[This is autobiography's] law of gravity: namely, that writing about his own existence ironically entails a denial of his existence as his own and therefore as a secure referential source for such writing.

Louis Renza, 1980

Sometimes, in a tired civilization like our own, it seems there is nothing left to pursue, that we can only repeat, with less resonance, what others have said definitively before us. Autobiography, however, is an area which has been largely ignored and positively invites fresh acts of imaginative and intellectual attention.

Peter Abbs, 1989

I began this book by advancing the claim that autobiography in education existed in an undertheorized state. However, this claim was not meant to imply that educators of various stripes have not brought forward reasons for its use that they found compelling. What it was meant to alert us to was that there exist additional ways of conceptualizing autobiography that have the potential to make current practices more powerful, even as these highly worked out conceptions offer the possibility of uncovering a new vocabulary of critique. The story of how these different conceptions of autobiography hang together, or might be made to hang together, within existing practices has provided the justification for undertaking this study. It is no accident, then, that the twists and turns of this story have veered between inspecting those educational sites where the largest and most comprehensive claims are being issued in the name of autobiography, and those where some fresh infusion of ideas might serve to advance the sophistication of its use, or at least serve as a reminder that such an objective is attainable should an educator so choose. What this final chapter is designed to accomplish is to suggest some ways by which we can move beyond conceiving the role of autobiography in education as an idiosyncratic mixture of history and fiction, or as a writerly project for reclaiming lost sources of intentionality, toward the kind of position that might prove capable of incorporating both of these aims within the strictures of a postmodern culture (Collins, 1989; Connor, 1989; Harvey, 1989).

With these final remarks, some attempt will be made to indicate what is at stake in seeking to move autobiography in education beyond common-sense conceptions of the form. Also, I want to ensure that the momentum gathered in the previous chapters contains sufficient energy to drive the kinds of conversations on autobiography that seem likely to prove valuable for educators in the near future. In order to go about this, it may well be stated in advance that I am going to sidle up to these concluding remarks in what may appear at first an oblique and, on the surface, unorthodox way. Therefore, in an effort at eschewing the seductions of teleology inherent in certain kinds of narratives, and consciously violating at least one long-hallowed rule of storytelling, some new characters, themes, plots, and possibilities will be introduced as autobiography in education looks toward the future.

THE CLAIMS OF NARRATIVE

In recent years, within an expanding number of disciplines and fields of inquiry, some heady claims have been put forward on behalf of the power of narrative. At the most fundamental and crudest level, one claim is that all knowledge derives from or partakes of a definite narrative thrust or interest. An example of this claim can be found in the work of historian Hayden White (1978), who maintains that history itself is a narrative construct, one whose meaning is produced by the "tropics of discourse" employed by the historian to bring shape and sense to a mass of undifferentiated material. Although we will return to White's ideas in another context later, at bottom his position can usefully be considered as part of a larger debate in the social sciences between positivism and humanism. In this instance Hekman (1986) captures the essence of the conflict well. She states that, following the Enlightenment conception of scientific knowledge, positivist thought has taken the position that "the goal of the social sciences is to gather 'objective data' and subject it to scientific analysis" (p. 168), whereas adherents of the humanist position accept as a given the subjective nature of all human understanding and argue instead that social science is subjective "because it deals with *meaningful* action" (p. 168, emphasis in original). In other words, the debate rests on the positivist assumption that if the facts are only set down in their proper order, then the "truth" will inevitably and surely stand revealed. For White and others of the humanist camp, this kind of thinking harbors the seeds of delusion. Not only is there always heated exchange over just what precisely the facts are, but even if there were agreement, their arrangement or construction could be plotted along different lines, a narrative undertaking that would largely depend upon the ideological worldview of the writer.

Likewise, when we turn to philosophy, and in particular to the work of Rorty (1982) and his idea of a post-Philosophical culture, we encounter the contention that although there have been many so-called revolutions in Philosophy (capital "P"), the same old problems remain on the agenda, a situation that places blinkers on analytic Philosophers and prevents them from recognizing that, as Rorty states (following Derrida), Philosophy is a kind of writing. Rorty argues that it is difficult to find something interesting to say about "Truth" anymore, and that the moral of his story is bound up with what he would see as the neopragmatist's answer to the fate of philosophy in general, namely, "that the best hope for philosophy is not to practice Philosophy" (p. xv). Philosophy must give up its omniscient narrator's role, its pretence of having access to a privileged Truth. This means an end to "Philosophy" and the birth of "philosophy" as an intellectually respectable undertaking, yet one that still has many interesting and useful narrative connections and interpretations to make among the various vocabularies within a culture. To commit oneself to this kind of philosophy is, as Rorty knows, not only to surrender those pronouncements that would claim a universal significance, but also to agree with Stanley Cavell that we must give up the "possibility that one among endless true descriptions of me tells who I am" (cited in Rorty, 1982, p. xl). The role of the philosopher in this post-Philosophical narrative is as a "conversational partner" (Rorty, 1979, p. 372), one whose purpose is to study "the comparative advantages and disadvantages of the various ways of talking which our race has invented" (Rorty, 1982, p. xl).

What I want to emerge from these thumbnail sketches is of some importance for my concluding remarks on autobiography in education, for they point first of all to the need to question, in typical poststructuralist fashion, the movement of this book itself as a narrative, one that could have been constructed along other lines with emphases centered around different points of interest. But second, and less archly, they also point to the need to inquire into how the various conversations, discourses, and vocabularies in education that take autobiography as their focus of attention have been played off one another in my own text, as well as to indicate how these conversations might be extended in a useful direction. Thus, this chapter should not be seen as a conclusion after the manner of a classic realist text in literature, with its inevitable move toward the closure (and disclosure) of that which has been concealed (see Belsey, 1980, p. 105 ff), but rather one that moves to reengage in another way with some of the issues that have been taken up in the course of reinterpreting the interpreters and reinterpreters. In this sense, then, my final chapter seeks to keep the conversation about the place of autobiography in education going by introducing new voices and by considering again what some familiar ones have to say in the light of these fresh conversational moves.

Autobiography Now

It might be argued with some fairness that the story this book has told about autobiography in education and the curriculum has been captured episodically as we visited each new site of inquiry. The selection and presentation of these sites or episodes, starting with elementary education and ending at curriculum theory, could also be interpreted as a value judgment, since a narrative structured this way might, in one view, represent a move from lesser to greater degrees of sophistication and awareness of its potential. On the other hand, the narrative might be interpreted ironically as telling a tale of missed opportunities, of the gap between promise and delivery, or between formal properties and transcendent claims. However one chooses to interpret this story, certain broad features have begun to make themselves plain, although none of them can be asserted with the kind of absolute conviction one might consider necessary to convince the skeptical.

First of all, autobiography, whether strictly or loosely defined, seems destined to play an important role in an increasing number of school subjects, for example, language education, the sciences, social studies, and health education, as a consequence of the stress now being placed generally in the curriculum on personalizing knowledge and privileging the students' stake in constructing knowledge on their own terms. This position seems generally in line with the movement in educational and curriculum theory toward a neopragmatist or constructivist epistemology, a view of knowledge creation to which I have alluded intermittently throughout, especially in Chapters 3 and 5 with respect to Dewey's work and to current research into teacher thinking and the understanding of a teacher's personal practical knowledge (Clandinin, 1985; Connelly & Clandinin, 1987).

Second, autobiography seems inevitably linked to several neo-Romantic projects that would take the nature of a student's self-understanding as their primary concern. Whether we decide to focus on the whole-language classroom in elementary education (Goodman, 1986), on preservice teacher education courses, or the use of *currere* as curriculum theory, the Romantic interest in the developing self of the student or teacher and in the struggle against societal and institutional constraints constitutes the kind of preoccupation with reading and writing the self that cuts across many disciplinary and subject fields. Third, the move toward self-narrative, in Bruner's (1987) understanding of the term, contains the potential to bring new poignancy to how educators come to view the relationship between margins and centers. For in spite of the inevitable feeling of alienation brought about by writing in the autobiographical mode, and in spite of the resistance to personal disclosure that many students show when requested to write personally, on an important level autobiography is working as an ancillary method in educational settings for marginalized groups like women and people of color as an example of what Freire (1970) calls *conscientization*, of seeing how subjectivity is constructed along differential relations of power, and hence of being placed in a position to effect meaningful change (Giroux, 1988; Goodson, 1985; Nias, 1989).

In other words, these tendencies support my general argument that autobiography in education takes part at every turn in the dialectical interplay between the construction of subjectivity as a project undertaken both collectively and socially, even as it explores and gives voice to those sedimented layers of individual consciousnesses that may have been buried or silenced under pressure from the dominant discourses and modes of representation in a culture (Roman, Christian-Smith, & Ellsworth, 1988).

But if these kinds of broad generalizations can be sustained or extracted from a narrative in which autobiography plays the role of liberating hero(ine) who assumes various forms of developmental disguise, there are certainly other aspects to this role that are far from clear and that can sustain some additional investigation. In other words, it has been assumed all along by most proponents of autobiography in education that the activity of reading and writing the self operates in two ways: from the inside out as an *expression* of a self already constituted, and from the outside in as a way of going to work on the self through the production and consumption of a *text*. But this problem of authorship conceals, as Sprinker (1980) would have it, "an intricate web of related problems" (p. 322), problems related to the apparently simple question "Who is X?" where "X" stands for the individual author of the autobiography. Although we have had some occasion to remark in Chapter 2 and elsewhere on the nature of autobiography as an essentially fictional undertaking, no time has been spent on the notion of authorship itself. Michel Foucault's essay "What Is an Author?" (1977) is pertinent at this point in that it raises crucial issues that are not mere arbitrary twists or subplots to our narrative, but that take us close to the heart of the dialectical movement between the individual and the group, as well as help us to visualize the possibility of a new and expanded role for autobiography in education and the curriculum.

The story Foucault tells has been responsible for the unsettling jolt experienced not only within literary studies but more widely throughout the humanities in general. For those of us in education its implications may in the long run prove equally unsettling, for as we will see, Foucault's ideas in fact come closest to describing certain largely unacknowledged trends in the use of autobiography in the educational initiatives we have been considering. First of all, however, it ought to be made clear that Foucault's argument could be construed as a form of intellectual mischief, since the concept of the author that Foucault challenges is one that lies close to our hearts and to the dictates of any common-sense understanding of the term we might care to propose. For most of us there would seem to be little use in doubting that the students whose writing we so conscientiously grade, and in whose margins we so assiduously make our comments and conduct our end of the dialogue, are not in fact the subjective presences who wrote the piece and who are ultimately responsible for its strengths or defects. The student writes the story or the research paper, then signs his or her name, certifying to its authenticity as the work of that author. Indeed, the existence of quotation marks is a material reminder of the belief that the origin of an idea in another person's consciousness should be acknowledged, while plagiarism itself can be defined as a crime against the author. But it is this question of origins, of locating the ultimate source of meaning in, say, the will of the individual, that has proved for some in the poststructuralist camp a real stumbling block. And although I can do little more than indicate the complexity of the idea here (for more extended treatment see Cherryholmes, 1988; Culler, 1982), the entire question of what constitutes an origin, what would count as marks of this presence, has proved the singular preoccupation of French philosophers like Barthes, Derrida, and Foucault in their attempt to deconstruct philosophy as a metaphysics of presence and to "decenter the subject."

As examples of familiar concepts that rely for their currency on the value of presence, we might wish to begin by considering Culler's (1982) list:

> . . . the immediacy of sensation, the presence of ultimate truths to a divine consciousness, the effective presence of an origin in a historical development, a spontaneous or unmediated intuition, . . . the presence in speech of logical and grammatical structures, truth as what subsists behind appearances, and the effective presence of a goal in the steps that lead to it. The authority of presence, its power of valorization, structures all our thinking. The notion of "making clear," "grasping," "demonstrating," "revealing," and "showing what is the case," all invoke presence. (pp. 93–94)

The ubiquitousness of concepts like these as they point to the way in which great value is placed on the individual willing subject, and on the sovereignty of authors over their work, is not only the common coin of our daily discourse, but also would seem to present a metaphysical court of last appeal as a bulwark against any assaults on our basic humanity. For example, if "I" am not the author of this book, or if our students are not the authors of their autobiographies and research papers, or if Shakespeare is not the author of *Hamlet*, then who (or what) is? Michael Sprinker (1980), in his comments as a literary theorist on the significance of the poststructuralist project for autobiography, provides this succinct answer, to which we would do well to attend before inspecting the specifics of Foucault's own response:

> Every text is an articulation of the relations between texts, a product of intertextuality, a weaving together of what has already been produced elsewhere in discontinuous form; every subject, every author, every self is the articulation of an intersubjectivity structured within and around the discourses available at any moment in time. (p. 325)

As we will see, the significance of intertextuality and intersubjectivity for what we would make of autobiography in education can hardly be overstressed. Although the story Foucault himself tells is indeed disruptive in that it interrogates all our deeply held assumptions about education as preeminently a humanistic undertaking, I would argue along with the poststructuralists that as paradoxical as it may seem, the antihumanism of poststructuralism may serve to move us toward a view of autobiography in education as an intertextual and intersubjective project, a project that presses hard against the positions of those who prefer to characterize autobiography as primarily the expression of a unique individual consciousness.

Foucault and the Idea of an Author

Foucault (1977) begins his influential essay "What Is an Author?" by setting aside "the sociohistorical analysis of the author as an individual" (p. 14) and instead wants to restrict himself to examining "the singular relationship that holds between an author and a text, the manner in which a text points to this figure who is outside and precedes it" (p. 14). He locates in the self-referentiality of much contemporary writing not only an effort to free writing from the Romantic legacy of Wordsworth's well-known "spontaneous overflow of powerful feelings," that is, with writing that somehow expresses the subjectivity of the author, but also an analysis of how writing "unfolds like a game that inevitably moves beyond its own rules and finally leaves them behind" (p. 15). This "voluntary obliteration of the self" (p. 15) is a sacrificial death that results in effacing from the text the individual characteristics of the writer. And as far as Foucault is concerned, the complete significance of this death of the author has never been fully appreciated for two reasons.

First, the whole notion of a writer's "work" has not been sufficiently problematized. There is a definite need to take into account the relationship between the death of the author and the so-called unity of everything the author wrote, "everything" here meaning not only his actual published pieces, but the drafts, revisions, doodlings, and marginalia that are "the millions of traces left by an individual after his death" (p. 16). Second, what Foucault calls *écriture* is also responsible for the continuing presence of the author and for preventing us from taking full account of his disappearance. *Écriture* is concerned neither with the act of writing nor with elaborating an author's meaning, but rather with understanding "the conditions of its spatial dispersal and its temporal deployment" (p. 16). In other words, the author, rather than having disappeared in the manner Foucault would have us consider, has been transformed by the workings of *écriture* into a kind of "transcendental anonymity" (p. 16), into something approaching the status of an immortal Other, such as in Shakespeare's Sonnet XVIII ("Shall I compare thee to a summer's day?"), the existence of the poem itself guaranteeing not only the immortality of the love object, but sustaining the notion of an author's presence after his death.

In opposition to these conceptions, which work to conceal the fact of the author's disappearance, Foucault would have us consider "the empty space" (p. 17) left by this disappearance in order to derive a more satisfactory understanding of the use of an author's name in legitimating different forms of *relationships* among texts. It is unnecessary to rehearse the entire course of Foucault's argument in this respect; the upshot and significance of his analysis of what, say, Kierkegaard's continuous use of so many pseudonyms in his works means is that "the author's name characterizes a particular manner of existence of discourse" (p. 17). In this way an author's name always remains "at the contours of texts" (p. 19) and indicates the existence and status of certain kinds of discourse within a culture. Thus, an author's name is a variable that accompanies certain kinds of texts and excludes others. In Foucault's (1977) examples, "a contract can have an underwriter, but not an author; . . . an anonymous poster attached to a wall may have a writer, but he cannot be an author" (p. 19). What, therefore, is the function of an author in the sense Foucault would like to valorize? That function is, he states, "to characterize the existence, circulation, and operation of certain discourses within a society" (p. 19).

The idea of an author as a function of discourse not only raises immediate problems and possibilities for conceptualizing autobiography within literary theory, but by extension presents an equal number of important issues regarding its use in education. For example, as we saw in Chapter 4, Britton's appeal to the work of Widdowson on the use of first-person pronouns in novels, stories, and poems drew our attention to the fact that the "I" in these instances need not refer directly to the writer, but rather to a kind of second self whose similarity to the writer, as Foucault reminds us, "is never fixed and undergoes considerable alteration within the course of a single book" (p. 23). In other words, the kind of discourse that supports this author-function is characterized by "a plurality of egos" (p. 23) who are not identical with the "I" who does the telling and narrating. Rather, these egos are dispersed throughout the discourse to give rise to "a series of subjective positions that individuals of any class may come to occupy" (p. 23). Autobiography in education and the curric-

ulum, then, taken under the preceding kinds of qualifications, constitutes a mode of discourse whose very function is to make problematic
the meaning of subjectivity within a culture. In addition, it lends incidental and powerful support to Gunn's earlier contention that we
might initially do well to consider autobiography as a mode of *reading*.
Reading, because as Sprinker (1980) informs us in his discussion of
Kierkegaard's pseudonyms, "Kierkegaard" is not an individual subject at all but rather "a multiplicity of subjects" (p. 332) whose knowledge of the meaning of his own works is only constructed as a reader,
a form of intersubjectivity "generated by the confrontation between
the discourse . . . and the interpretative responses . . . made by Kierkegaard as a reader of that discourse" (p. 323). The import of this for
education is that as autobiography in its many guises and varieties is
inserted into the cultural formations of classrooms in schools and colleges, this dispersal of the author-function strips subjectivity of its
transcendental mystique and reconstitutes it "as a complex and variable function of discourse" (Foucault, 1977, p. 28).

By textualizing self-knowledge in this way, teachers might be
brought to understand that requests to students to produce work that
reeks of "authenticity," "sincerity," and discloses privileged glimpses
into the human heart (to name only the more obvious neo-Romantic
concepts) are part of a series of requests that operate from a conception of a freestanding subject who somehow originates ex nihilo texts
that are the equivalent of a unique set of fingerprints. Foucault would
have us suspend these types of requests; in their place he would have
us ask a set of alternative questions, ones that strike at the core of any
claims we might wish to make for autobiography itself: "Through
what forms can an entity like the subject appear in the order of discourse . . . what rules does it follow in each type of discourse?" (p.
28); " 'Where does it [discourse] come from; how is it circulated; who
controls it?' 'What placements are determined for possible subjects?' "
(p. 29). Questions like these are disturbing for teachers and what they
might make of their classrooms, since they serve to cast a long
shadow over the premises regarding common-sense notions of the
self or of the existence of a transcendental ego in the manner espoused by many advocates of autobiography in educational settings.
As an instance of the way in which Foucault's ideas can initiate fresh
thinking on the discursive practices within a field of inquiry, I want to
turn to the project of the New Literacy in language education based
on the work of theorists like Britton, Graves, Smith, and others. And
it is to review briefly again this episode in the light of our discussion
of Foucault, as well as to examine further possibilities for autobiogra-

phy conceptualized from a poststructuralist position, that we now turn.

NARRATION AND THE SUBJECT OF DISCOURSE

Throughout the analysis of the contribution made by Britton to situating a concern for autobiography and personal expressive writing in education, a concept of the child-as-artist emerged as a consequence of stressing the function language played in the child's search for meaning. This constructivist position was upheld not only by appeals to the work of cognitive psychologists like Bruner, but gained its greatest educational currency in the work of Dewey and in the philosophy and methods of progressive education in general. Although Willinsky (1987) has made a good case for tracing the roots of the New Literacy back to the nineteenth-century Romantic project, with its concern for organicism and process as well as "the centrality of self and imagination" (p. 286) as first principles, I would want to stress even more forcefully that there is a contradiction in the nature of the mechanism that drives New Literacy classrooms. This contradiction lies in the foregrounding of the *group* process at work, even as the Romantic concept of the artist is held out for students to emulate as these budding authors sign their names to an increasing library of their own published works. In this instance, the politics of pedagogy would seem to be at odds with the ideology of individualism. On the one hand, as Willinsky (1987) puts it in commenting on a major feature of the New Literacy, its greatest advance "has been to extend and democratize our concept of the mind's powers until it has become the right of every child to lay claim to a kind of unconscious genius which requires only a writerly opportunity to bring it into play" (p. 275). In other words, there could be no clearer example of an educational endeavor that takes up so forcibly the project of self-construction, of the individual student's ability to write the self as the major purpose of the autobiographical impulse and of expressive writing generally.

On the other hand, when we begin to take Foucault seriously, it is not that for all practical purposes the names on the covers of our students' work should be taken, as Derrida would have it, under "erasure," but that the teacher should reconceptualize the classroom as a social and cultural formation where many forms of discourse are brought into existence, circulated, and controlled, and where what is revealed in the students' writing may be less an expression of an original and originating subjectivity than, as Goldman (1977) states, "a collective and trans-individual one" (p. 29). What, therefore, the students' works "express," where "the author" of this writing is to be found, is in the unpredictable influence of pieces of literature as other voices in the classroom conversation, in the various ideas generated and shared by the existence of ongoing conferences with fellow students and teachers, and in the many traces and fragments of discourses provided by the availability of music, film, video, and posters. In other words, it is not just at the level of a high cultural artifact that we can observe the writer's self emerge as an imminent construction from the number of discourses that make up the "text" of a Rousseau, Nabokov, or Henry Adams. On the more homely level of the school the parallel holds good also, as teachers observe and guide Johnny and Suzie in their collective aesthetic struggle to shape their own narratives of experience. What our reading of Foucault makes clear is that we as educators must become more aware that what we are witnessing in our reconceptualized classrooms may not be the manifest signs of an ego that is already constituted in various ways. Rather, we must begin to insist that because the range of subject positions from which children can understand themselves and their relation to culture is altered across a number of discourses (novels, poetry, film, other students' writing), the students' view of themselves is both challenged and confirmed in often contradictory ways.

Consequently, when there exists a clear dialectical relationship between individuals and the discourses in which their subjectivity is constructed and represented, then an educational endeavor like the New Literacy stands to gain immeasurably by acknowledging the contradictoriness of some of its own theory and practice. This is not to suggest, however, that by embracing a poststructuralist reading of New Literacy noncontradictory patterns and procedures are set to take over; rather, it is to suggest that the promotion of the Romantic figure of the child-as-artist has overshadowed the social and intersubjective nature of literacy learning and has perpetuated the ideology of writing as preeminently a form of individual self-expression.

Another major issue Foucault's essay raises so clearly that is important not only for the New Literacy but for education as a whole is the nature of control, of the relationship between power and knowledge. As was indicated briefly in Chapter 1 and earlier in this chapter, it is axiological for writers such as Anyon (1979), Apple (1979, 1983), and other advocates of the new sociology of education that knowledge is ideological and is legitimated by the discursive practices of people like textbook publishers and held in place by what Louis Althusser (1971) calls the "Ideological State Apparatus" of the school.

As many commentators, including Carroll (1988), Cherryholmes (1988), Silverman (1980), and others have shown, in Althusser's view ideology obscures and discourages a complete understanding of the real conditions of our existence by normalizing and causing to appear as coherent that which is in fact contradictory and open to contestation. According to Althusser (1971), the focal point of ideology is the individual to the extent that *"all ideology has the function (which defines it) of 'constituting' concrete individuals as subjects"* (p. 160, original emphasis). This immediately poses as problematic the relationship between ideology and language, in that questions of identity, from the point of view of poststructuralism, are bound up with the subject-positions discourses of all kinds offer the individual. It is here, then, that the new questions Foucault would have us ask become even more germane. Where discourses come from, how they are circulated, and who controls them are large and not easily answered; but they do point toward the necessity of "rethinking the subject," as this designation refers to the idea of an individual and to the way knowledge is abstracted and organized for use in schools.

These ideas may seem a far cry from our students' constructing their journals and autobiographical narratives in our classrooms. But what they point to is quite simply the extent to which we are willing to believe that our acts of intervention in the classroom to minimize the workings of teacher power will prove crucial for our students. Whether through simple acts of rearranging the furniture, or by more complex acts of coming out from behind the desk, as Atwell (1987) does to position herself in the middle of student conferences; or again by keeping the conversation alive among different and competing discourses and forms of representation that are introduced into the classroom, procedures like these stand the best chance of creating the conditions under which students come collectively to understand some of the workings of ideology and power and their relation to the construction of self and culture.

Yet even if many of these kinds of abstractions could somehow be stripped away, what still remains in discussing the future of autobiography in education is the conflict centered around the contentious (and no less abstract) issue of the self and which versions or arguments regarding its nature and construction educators will continue to find most appealing. In general, as a working principle that cuts across all of the educational sites I have inspected, the self that most educators are concerned we get closer in touch with is some permutation of Husserl's transcendental ego, that is, a unique self that exists across time, the essence of our Being. What we might call the surface configurations of personality, character, and the like serve only as a mask, a cover for the essential self that is to be located "inside" us, traditionally in Western cultures somewhere between the eyes and inside the head. The argument here is that whether autobiography enters the curriculum in elementary school, or later in the narratives of educational experience demanded of pre- and in-service teachers, its prime function is to make memory speak, to cause students to become increasingly conscious of the ties that bind them to culture and society, and to help them discover valuable aspects of their "true" selves. It is this conception of the self that the educators discussed in Chapters 5 and 6 advanced to support their own practice of autobiographical method. Yet even when they themselves are willing to recognize the fictive nature of that self, many still cling to its transcendent qualities in the religious or spiritual belief that this self is another word for soul.

In similar fashion, Dewey, even though he largely borrowed Mead's conception of the self as a social construction, and seemed content to argue for the practical necessity of education as the way toward creating the conditions for self-realization, could at other moments still be found casting a longing eye in the direction of Plato and his transcendent Forms (see Dewey, 1960a, p. 13). The same is true for some contemporary educators who, like Dewey and the teachers of the New Literacy who rely on his thinking, find themselves in that contradictory position alluded to earlier. On the one hand, they realize that the inquiry into the self and its history is always hedged within the limits imposed by writing and the production of text, while on the other hand, they seem to draw back from wholly embracing the unsettling conclusions brought about by their own reasoning. Our discussion of Foucault allows us to state this in another way, namely, that this struggle over the self, and hence over the legitimation of discourses like autobiography that would reveal that self to itself, is fundamentally an issue regarding "whose" self we are at any one time referring to: the essential self of the phenomenologists, or the discursive, constructed self of the poststructuralists.

I am alive to the fact that neopragmatists like Rorty are currently lining themselves up within the poststructuralist camp because they see the move toward deconstruction and poststructuralism as part of the logic inherent within the pragmatic agenda, and that pragmatism itself is compatible with this "deconstructive turn" (see Norris, 1985, pp. 139–166). In fact, Rorty himself has attempted to unite Dewey and Foucault in an alliance against both positivists and idealists (1982, p. xlii). What needs stressing here, however, is that the educational legacy of a figure like Dewey has allowed generations of educators to promote the project of self-realization and its epistemological consequences as, like the poststructuralist project, always provisional, always part of an ongoing social and collective process. In spite of this, what has also remained as a permanent feature of Dewey's legacy is the nostalgic impulse toward idealism, an impulse that has allowed prominent language educators like Britton, Graves, and Smith to continue to promote the perennially beguiling and Romantic notion of the child-as-artist: the author, origin, and endpoint of this discourse of the self.

The moment has come, therefore, if not for the kinds of wholesale revisions that would be consistent with the logic of much of the espoused (Deweyan) theory that the New Literacy advances to support its practices, then for beginning to entertain the possibility that as Weintraub earlier pointed out, each new age or epoch demands a new image of selfhood, one more in keeping with the way that age conceives of itself. Whether this will turn out to be some version of Lasch's (1984) "minimal self" remains to be seen; what is clear is that as self-conscious writers from Vico to Nabokov and most recently Updike (1989), whose name for this plurality of selves is "our disposable ancestors" (p. 221), have always known, not only does "the origin and end of autobiography converge in the very act of writing" (Sprinker, 1980, p. 342), but the autobiographical act of personal discovery also lays bare the depth and extent of our connections to a larger collectivity.

CONCLUSION

But what kind of writing might this look like in educational contexts where teachers find themselves intuitively drawn toward making provision for the fruits of self-discovery in their students, but also find themselves constrained by the age and abilities of the would-be autobiographers, as well as many features of our postmodern world and culture that are working silently on us (Collins, 1989; Fiske, 1989)? Perhaps I might begin to point a way toward answering that question by echoing the sentiments of historian Hayden White, whose point of view encapsulates many of the tensions and possibilities raised in this chapter.

White chides modern historiographers for their failure to adopt the full range of contemporary narrative modes and options. They, like many of the educators we have discussed, still continue to conceive of narrative in its nineteenth-century realist phase, in which it followed the strictures of chronological sequence. By turning their backs on the modes of writing made available to us in the work of modern and postmodern writers, historiographers have trapped themselves within a tradition of writing that may now be irrelevant, as well as ignoring the possibilities for exploring alternative methods of representation, methods which, while we should not minimize their often extreme difficulty, nevertheless open up future avenues for educational research and experimentation. White (1978) concludes:

> When many historians speak of 'art' . . . they seem to mean that they are artists in the way that Scott or Thackeray were artists. . . . [It is] as if they believed that the major, not to say the sole, purpose of art is to tell a story. . . . It is of course true that the artist's purpose *may* be served by telling a story, but this is only one of the possible modes of representation offered to him today, and it is a decreasingly important one at that, as the *nouveau roman* in France has so impressively shown. (pp. 42–43)

Now while we in education might not wish to sound so polemical or appear so sanguine with respect to the possibilities for the adoption of postmodern techniques in language education or in education generally, the fact that there exist a number of alternative literary modes of self-representation does leave the way open for empirical studies that take as their object the processes involved in experimenting with narrative and metanarrative modes of writing. Such initiatives are premised of course on exposing professors, researchers, teachers, and students to a range of creative works as examples of the kinds of writing techniques that also could conceivably be brought to the task of reconstituting the practice of autobiography in education along poststructural lines. And if this may appear too fanciful and utopian for some, for others it might prove a fruitful line of research given our awareness of the lag time between advances at the forefront of literature and criticism and the likelihood of their influence on teacher education courses or on school curricula.

　　To sum up, then, in the theorizing and discussions put forward in the course of this book I have tried not only to give a feeling for the kinds of unacknowledged problems that adhere to the use of autobiography, but also for the existence of the real possibilities that the present chapter has shown still lie untapped within the genre and that can provide fertile areas for future theorizing and research, as, for example, Lejeune's (1989) recent essay on the "ghostwritten" autobiography makes clear. However, as we have seen throughout, the use of autobiography is always fraught with a certain number of drawbacks, particularly when instructors or researchers themselves take a naive realist's view and continue to believe that their students' and teachers' autobiographies are or ought to be considered true in some easily verifiable way.

On the level of school program, however, there is reason to believe that there is a movement afoot to have at least the reading of autobiographies occupy a more significant position within a subject like social studies than it appears to do at present. For example, Krass (1989), in the context of civics education in the United States, seems to be on the right track as she makes an interesting case for the use of autobiography in civics courses "as an instrument for fostering public spiritedness" (p. 104), a recognition of the potent social or collective dimension to its use. Her agenda, though laudable, may at first glance seem to ask a great deal, since she offers the reading of autobiography as a nostrum against the ills of materialism, presentism, individualism, conformity, and mediocrity, all of which she believes are endemic within present-day American society. Although this sounds more like a task for genetic engineering than for the reading and discussion of exemplary autobiographies in the interpretive community of the classroom, we would hope her new generation of social studies teachers will at least be alive to the fact that they are dealing with a very complex and demanding genre, one that does not always wear its intentions on its sleeve and that can yet contain a wealth of riches, some of which will become apparent to both themselves and their students alike only very slowly over time.

Finally, if we are to judge by the productive manner in which autobiography has been taken up in diverse educational settings by women's groups, feminist theorists, and ethnic and racial minorities as one of the most powerful methods for reclaiming their collective voices and for redeeming a lost sense of historical consciousness (Steedman, 1986), then it behooves all of us who are involved in whatever aspects of public education to begin to consider the extent of our own knowledge and attitudes toward autobiography and its potential as well.

Protean, multifaceted, and slippery as the genre surely is, this chapter has suggested some new directions for autobiography in education even as the book itself has demonstrated both the pitfalls and promises that lie in store for us as we take up our pens, processors, and paint and ask our students to take up theirs and begin to construct our autobiographies together.

References

Abbs, P. (1976). *Root and blossom: Essays on the philosophy, practice and politics of English teaching.* London: Heinemann.

Abbs, P. (1977). English teaching: An expressive discipline. *English in Education, 11*(3), 48–56.

Abbs, P. (1979). *Reclamations.* London: Heinemann.

Abbs, P. (1989). *Aa is for aesthetic.* London: Falmer Press.

Allen, D. (1980). *English teaching since 1965: How much growth?* London: Heinemann.

Althusser, L. (1971). *Lenin and philosophy and other essays* (B. Brewster, trans.). London: New Left Books.

Anyon, J. (1979). Ideology and U.S. history textbooks. *Harvard Educational Review, 49*(3): 361–386.

Apple, M. W. (1979). *Ideology and curriculum.* London: Routledge and Kegan Paul.

Apple, M. W. (1983). *Education and power.* London: Routledge and Kegan Paul.

Applebee, A. (1980). *The child's concept of story.* Chicago: University of Chicago Press.

Atwell, N. (1987). *In the middle: Writing, reading, and learning with adolescents.* Montclair, NJ: Boynton/Cook.

Ball, S. (1988). Relations, structure and conditions in curriculum change: A political history of English teaching 1970–85. In I. Goodson (Ed.), *International perspectives on the curriculum* (pp. 17–45). London: Croom Helm.

Barnes, D., Barnes, D., & Clarke, S. (1984). *Versions of English.* London: Heinemann.

Barthes, R. (1977). *Image, music, text.* Glasgow: Fontana.

Belsey, C. (1980). *Critical practice.* London: Methuen.

Benstock, S. (1988). *The private self: Theory and practice of women's autobiographical writings.* Chapel Hill: University of North Carolina Press.

Berman, M. (1988). *All that is solid melts into air: The experience of modernity.* New York: Penguin.

Bernstein, R. J. (1960). Introduction. In R. J. Bernstein (Ed.), *On experience, nature, and freedom* (pp. ix–xlvii). New York: Liberal Arts Press.

Blewett, J. (1960). *John Dewey: His thought and influence.* New York: Fordham University Press.

Bottrall, M. (1958). *Every man a phoenix: Studies in seventeenth-century autobiography.* Chester Springs, PA: Dufour.

Bowers, C. A. (1969). *The progressive educator and the Depression: The radical years.* New York: Random House.

Brent, A. (1978). *Philosophical foundations for the curriculum.* London: George Allen & Unwin.

Britton, J. (1963). Literature. In J. Britton (Ed.), *The arts and current trends in education* (pp. 34–61). London: Evans Brothers.

Britton, J. (1970a). *Language and learning.* Harmondsworth: Penguin Books.

Britton, J. (1970b). Their language and our teaching. *English in Education, 4*(2), 5–13.

Britton, J. (1981). English teaching: Prospect and retrospect. *English in Education, 15*(2), 2–10.

Britton, J. (1982a). Spectator role and the beginnings of writing. In G. M. Pradl (Ed.), *Prospect and retrospect* (pp. 46–67). Montclair, NJ: Boynton/ Cook.

Britton, J. (1982b). How we got here. In G. M. Pradl (Ed.), *Prospect and retrospect* (pp. 169–184). Montclair, NJ: Boynton/Cook.

Britton, J. (1983). Writing and the story world. In B. Kroll & G. Wells (Eds.), *Explorations in the development of writing* (pp. 3–30). Chichester, England: John Wiley.

Brooks, C. (1947). *The well-wrought urn.* New York: Harcourt, Brace, Jovanovich.

Brown, T. M. (1988). How fields change: A critique of the "Kuhnian" view. In W. F. Pinar (Ed.), *Contemporary curriculum discourses* (pp. 18–30). Scottsdale, AZ: Gorsuch Scarisbrick.

Bruner, J. (1979). *On knowing: Essays for the left hand.* Cambridge: Harvard University Press.

Bruner, J. (1986). *Actual minds, possible worlds.* Cambridge: Harvard University Press.

Bruner, J. (1987). Life as narrative. *Social Research, 54*(1), 11–32.

Bruss, E. (1976). *Autobiographical acts.* Baltimore: Johns Hopkins University Press.

Burns, R. (1982). The need to problematise educational knowledge. In R. Goodings, M. Byram, & M. McPartland (Eds.), *Changing priorities in teacher education* (pp. 85–100). London: Croom Helm.

Butt, R. L., & Raymond, D. (1987). Arguments for using qualitative approaches in understanding teacher thinking: The case for biography. *Journal of Curriculum Theorizing, 7*(1), 62–93.

Butt, R. L., & Raymond, D. (1989). Studying the nature and development of teachers' knowledge using collaborative autobiography. In M. Huberman (Ed.), *International Journal of Educational Research, 13*(4), 403–419.

Butt, R. L., Raymond, D., & Yamagishi, L. (1988). Autobiographic praxis: Studying the formation of teachers' knowledge. *Journal of Curriculum Theorizing, 7*(4), 87–164.

Carlock, M. S. (1970). Humpty-Dumpty and the autobiography. *Genre, 3*(3), 340–350.

Carroll, N. (1988). *Mystifying movies: Fads and fallacies in contemporary film theory.* New York: Columbia University Press.

Cassirer, E. (1944). *An essay on man.* New Haven: Yale University Press.

Cherryholmes, C. H. (1988). *Power and criticism: Poststructural investigations in education.* New York: Teachers College Press.

Clandinin, D. J. (1985). Personal practical knowledge: A study of teachers' classroom images. *Curriculum Inquiry, 15*(4), 361–385.

Clandinin, D. J. (1986). *Classroom practice: Teacher images in action.* London: Falmer Press.

Collins, J. (1989). *Uncommon cultures: Popular culture and post-modernism.* New York: Routledge.

Connelly, M. F., & Clandinin, D. J. (1987). On narrative method, biography and narrative unities in the study of teaching. *Journal of Educational Thought, 21*(3), 130–139.

Connor, S. (1989). *Postmodernist culture: An introduction to theories of the contemporary.* Oxford: Basil Blackwell.

Cremin, L. (1961). *The transformation of the school: Progressivism in American education 1876–1957.* New York: Vintage Books.

Culler, J. (1982). *On deconstruction: Theory and criticism after structuralism.* Ithaca: Cornell University Press.

Dewey, J. (1929). *My pedagogic creed.* Washington: The Progressive Education Association.

Dewey, J. (1932). *Ethics* (2nd ed.). New York: Henry Holt.

Dewey, J. (1933). *How we think.* Boston: Heath and Company. (Original work published 1910)

Dewey, J. (1938). *Experience and education.* New York: Macmillan.

Dewey, J. (1958). *Experience and nature.* New York: Dover Publications. (Original work published 1925)

Dewey, J. (1960a). From absolutism to experimentalism. In R. J. Bernstein (Ed.), *On experience, nature and freedom* (pp. 3–18). New York: Liberal Arts Press.

Dewey, J. (1960b). Time and individuality. In R. J. Bernstein (Ed.), *On experience, nature, and freedom* (pp. 224–243). New York: Liberal Arts Press.

Dewey, J. (1963). *The child and the curriculum.* Chicago: Chicago University Press. (Original work published 1902)

Dewey, J. (1964). *Democracy and education.* New York: Macmillan. (Original work published 1916)

Dewey, J. (1967). *The school and society.* Chicago: University of Chicago Press. (Original work published 1900)

Dewey, J. (1980). *Art as experience.* New York: Putnam. (Original work published 1934)

Dewey, J., & Bentley, A. F. (1949). *Knowing and the known.* Boston: Beacon Press.

Dixon, J. (1967). *Growth through English.* Oxford: Oxford University Press.

Dodd, P. (1987). History or fiction: Balancing contemporary autobiography's claims. *Mosaic, 20*(4), 61–69.

Doyle, B. (1989). *English and Englishness.* London: Methuen.

Eakin, P. J. (1985). *Fictions in autobiography: Studies in the art of self-invention.* Princeton: Princeton University Press.

Earle, W. (1977). *Autobiographical consciousness.* Chicago: Chicago University Press.

Eisner, E. (1982). *Cognition and curriculum.* New York: Longman.

Egan, K. (1988). *Primary understanding.* New York: Routledge.

Egan, S. (1984). *Patterns of experience in autobiography.* Chapel Hill: University of North Carolina Press.

Fenstermacher, G. (1986). Philosophy of research on teaching: Three aspects. In M. C. Wittrock (Ed.), *Handbook of research on teaching* (3rd ed.) (pp. 37–49). New York: Macmillan.

Fish, S. (1980). *Is there a text in this class?* Cambridge: Harvard University Press.

Fiske, J. (1989). *Understanding popular culture.* Boston: Unwin Hyman.

Fleishman, A. (1983). *Figures of autobiography: The language of self-writing in Victorian and modern England.* Berkeley: University of California Press.

Foucault, M. (1977). What is an author? *Screen, 1,* 13–33.

Freire, P. (1970). *Pedagogy of the oppressed.* New York: Continuum Press.

Freund, E. (1987). *The return of the reader: Reader-response criticism.* London: Methuen.

Friedman, S. S. (1988). Women's autobiographical selves: Theory and practice. In S. Benstock (Ed.), *The private self: Theory and practice of women's autobiographical writings* (pp. 34–62). Chapel Hill: University of North Carolina Press.

Frye, N. (1957). *The anatomy of criticism.* Princeton: Princeton University Press.

Frye, N. (1988). *On education.* Toronto: Fitzhenry & Whiteside.

Geuss, R. (1981). *The idea of a critical theory: Habermas and the Frankfurt school.* Cambridge: Cambridge University Press.

Giroux, H. A. (1983). *Theory and resistance in education: A pedagogy for the opposition.* South Hadley, MA: Bergin & Garvey.

Giroux, H. A. (1988). *Schooling and the struggle for public life: Critical pedagogy in the modern age.* Minneapolis: University of Minnesota Press.

Goldman, L. (1977). A discussion with Michel Foucault. *Screen, 1,* 29–33.

Goodman, K. (1986). *What's whole in whole language.* Richmond Hill, Ontario: Scholastic Press.

Goodson, I. (1985). *Teachers' lives and careers.* London: Falmer Press.

Gorman, G. (1988). *GCSE: A guide for parents, employers and candidates.* London: Kogan Page.

Graham, R. J. (1989). Autobiography and education. *Journal of Educational Thought, 23*(2), 92–105.

Gray, R. (1982). Autobiography now. *Kenyon Review, 4,* 31–55.

Greene, D. (1968). The use of autobiography in the eighteenth century. In P. B. Dahglian (Ed.), *Essays in eighteenth-century biography* (pp. 43–66). Bloomington: Indiana University Press.

Greene, M. (1975). Curriculum and consciousness. In W. Pinar (Ed.), *Curriculum theorizing: The reconceptualists* (pp. 299–317). Berkeley: McCutchan.

Grumet, M. R. (1976a). Existential and phenomenological foundations. In W. F. Pinar & M. R. Grumet, *Toward a poor curriculum* (pp. 31–50). Dubuque, IA: Kendall Hunt.

Grumet, M. R. (1976b). Toward a poor curriculum. In W. F. Pinar & M. R. Grumet, *Toward a poor curriculum* (pp. 67–88). Dubuque, IA: Kendall Hunt.

Grumet, M. R. (1976c). Psychoanalytic foundations. In W. F. Pinar & M. R. Grumet, *Toward a poor curriculum* (pp. 111–146). Dubuque, IA: Kendall Hunt.

Grumet, M. R. (1976d). Teachers' training seminar. 1975. In W. F. Pinar & M. R. Grumet, *Toward a poor curriculum* (pp. 147–174). Dubuque, IA: Kendall Hunt.

Grumet, M. R. (1981). Restitution and reconstruction of educational experience: An autobiographical method for curriculum theory. In M. Lawn & L. Barton (Eds.), *Rethinking curriculum studies* (pp. 115–130). London: Croom Helm.

Grumet, M. R. (1987). The politics of personal knowledge. *Curriculum Inquiry, 17*(3), 319–329.

Gunn, J. (1982). *Autobiography: Towards a poetics of experience.* Philadelphia: University of Pennsylvania Press.

Gusdorf, G. (1980). Conditions and limits of autobiography. In J. Olney (Ed.), *Autobiography: Essays theoretical and critical* (pp. 28–48). Princeton: Princeton University Press.

Habermas, J. (1971). *Knowledge and human interests* (J. Shapiro, trans.) Boston: Beacon Press.

Harding, D. W. (1937). The role of the onlooker. *Scrutiny, 6*(3), 247–258.

Harding, D. W. (1962). Psychological processes in the reading of fiction. *British Journal of Aesthetics, 2*, 133–147.

Hart, F. R. (1970). Notes for an anatomy of modern autobiography. *New Literary History, 1*, 485–511.

Harvey, D. (1989). *The condition of postmodernity: An enquiry into the origins of cultural change.* Oxford: Basil Blackwell.

Hekman, S. J. (1986). *Hermeneutics and the sociology of knowledge.* Oxford: Polity Press.

Hirsch, E. D. (1987). *Cultural literacy: What every American needs to know.* Boston: Houghton Mifflin.

Hirst, P. H. (1974). *Knowledge and the curriculum.* London: Routledge & Kegan Paul.

Holbrook, D. (1961). *English for maturity.* Cambridge: Cambridge University Press.

Holland, N. H. (1980). Unity identity text self. In J. P. Tompkins (Ed.), *Reader-response criticism: From formalism to post-structuralism* (pp. 118–133). Baltimore: Johns Hopkins University Press.

Hopkins, D. (1985). Drift and the problem of change in Canadian teacher education. In D. Hopkins & K. Reid (Eds.), *Rethinking teacher education* (pp. 107–129). London: Croom Helm.

Howarth, W. L. (1980). Some principles of autobiography. In J. Olney (Ed.), *Autobiography: Essays theoretical and critical* (pp. 84–114). Princeton: Princeton University Press.

Huebner, D. (1975). The tasks of the curriculum theorist. In W. F. Pinar (Ed.), *Curriculum theorizing: The reconceptualists* (pp. 250–270). Berkeley: McCutchan.

Jackson, P. (1981). Curriculum and its discontents. In H. A. Giroux, A. N. Penna, & W. F. Pinar (Eds.), *Curriculum and instruction: Alternatives in education* (pp. 367–381). Berkeley: McCutchan.

Kelly, G. (1963). *A theory of personality.* New York: Norton.

Krall, F. (1988). From the inside out: Personal history as educational research. *Educational Theory, 38*(4), 467–479.

Krass, A. (1989). Autobiographers as teachers: Towards solving the problem of civic education. In P. W. Jackson & S. Hartounian-Gordon (Eds.), *From Socrates to software: The teacher as text and the text as teacher* (pp. 90–114). Chicago: University of Chicago Press.

Kuhn, T. S. (1970). *The structure of scientific revolutions* (2nd ed.). Chicago: University of Chicago Press.

Langer, S. (1960). *Philosophy in a new key.* Cambridge: Harvard University Press.

Lanham, R. (1976). *The motives of eloquence.* New Haven: Yale University Press.

Lasch, C. (1978). *The culture of narcissism: American life in an age of diminishing expectations.* New York: W. W. Norton.

Lasch, C. (1984). *The minimal self.* New York: W. W. Norton.

Lawton, D. & Chitty, C. (1988). *The national curriculum.* London: University of London Institute of Education.

Lejeune, P. (1975). *Le pacte autobiographique.* Paris: Editions du Seuil.

Lejeune, P. (1989). *On autobiography.* Minneapolis: University of Minnesota Press.

Lifson, M. R. (1979). The myth of the fall: A description of autobiography. *Genre, 12*(1), 45–69.

Light, D. (1983). Culture and civilization: The politics of English teaching. *English in Education, 17*(1), 65–75.

MacDonald, J. B. (1975). Curriculum theory. In W. Pinar (Ed.), *Curriculum theorizing: The reconceptualists* (pp. 5–13). Berkeley: McCutchan.

Maguire, M., & Washington, S. (1983). London looks at English theory: Hurry up, please, it's time! *Highway One, 6*(2), 24–33.

Mathieson, M. (1975). *The preachers of culture.* London: Unwin.

Mazlisch, B. (1970). Autobiography and psycho-analysis: Between truth and self-deception. *Encounter, 35*, 28–37.

McKeon, R. (1951). Philosophy and action. *Ethics, 62*(2), 79–100.

McNeil, J. D. (1985). *Curriculum: A comprehensive introduction* (3rd ed.). Boston: Little, Brown.

Mead, G. H. (1959). *Mind, self and society.* Chicago: University of Chicago Press.

Mehlman, J. (1974). *A structural study of autobiography: Proust, Sartre, Leiris, Levi-Strauss.* Ithaca: Cornell University Press.

Morgan, R. (1978). *Going too far: The personal chronicle of a feminist.* New York: Vintage Books.

Nias, J. (1989). *Primary teachers talking: A study of teaching as work.* London: Routledge.

Norris, C. (1985). *The contest of faculties.* London: Methuen.

Oakley, A. (1981). *Subject women.* New York: Pantheon Books.

Olney, J. (1972). *Metaphors of self: The meaning of autobiography.* Princeton: Princeton University Press.

Olney, J. (Ed.). (1980). *Autobiography: Essays theoretical and critical.* Princeton: Princeton University Press.

Ornstein, A. C., & Hunkins, F. P. (1988). *Curriculum: Foundations, principles and issues.* New York: Prentice-Hall.

Pascal, R. (1960). *Design and truth in autobiography.* Cambridge: Harvard University Press.

Peters, R. S. (1966). *Ethics and education.* London: George Allen & Unwin.

Pinar, W. F. (1975a). Sanity, madness and the school. In W. F. Pinar (Ed.), *Curriculum theorizing: The reconceptualists* (pp. 359–383). Berkeley: McCutchan.

Pinar, W. F. (1975b). The analysis of educational experience. In W. F. Pinar (Ed.), *Curriculum theorizing: The reconceptualists* (pp. 384–395). Berkeley: McCutchan.

Pinar, W. F. (1975c). Currere: Towards reconceptualization. In W. F. Pinar (Ed.), *Curriculum theorizing: The reconceptualists* (pp. 396–414). Berkeley: McCutchan.

Pinar, W. F. (1975d). Search for a method. In W. F. Pinar (Ed.), *Curriculum theorizing: The reconceptualists* (pp. 415–424). Berkeley: McCutchan.

Pinar, W. F. (1981). A reply to my critics. In H. A. Giroux, A. N. Penna, & W. F. Pinar (Eds.), *Curriculum and instruction: Alternatives in education* (pp. 392–399). Berkeley: McCutchan.

Pinar, W. F. (Ed.). (1988a). *Contemporary curriculum discourses.* Scottsdale, AZ: Gorsuch Scarisbrick.

Pinar, W. F. (1988b). Introduction. In W. F. Pinar (Ed.), *Contemporary curriculum discourses* (pp. 1–13). Scottsdale, AZ: Gorsuch Scarisbrick.

Pinar, W. F., & Grumet, M. R. (1976). *Toward a poor curriculum.* Dubuque, IA: Kendall Hunt.

Polanyi, M. (1962). *Personal knowledge: Towards a postcritical philosophy.* New York: Harper.

Posner, G. J. (1988). Models of curriculum planning. In L. E. Beyer & M. W. Apple (Eds.), *The curriculum: Problems, politics, and possibilities* (pp. 77–97). Albany: State University of New York Press.

Postman, N., & Weingartner, C. (1969). *Teaching as a subversive activity.* New York: Delacorte Press.

Quinton, A. (1977). Dewey's theory of knowledge. In R. S. Peters (Ed.), *John Dewey reconsidered* (pp. 1–17). London: Routledge and Kegan Paul.

Renza, L. (1980). The veto of the imagination: A theory of autobiography. In J. Olney (Ed.), *Autobiography: Essays theoretical and critical* (pp. 268–295). Princeton: Princeton University Press.

Rieff, P. (1959). *Freud: The mind of the moralist*. Chicago: University of Chicago Press.

Roman, L., Christian-Smith, L., & Ellsworth, E. (1988). *Becoming feminine: The politics of popular culture*. London: Falmer Press.

Rorty, R. (1979). *Philosophy and the mirror of nature*. Princeton: Princeton University Press.

Rorty, R. (1982). *Consequences of pragmatism: Essays 1972–1980*. Minneapolis: University of Minnesota Press.

Rosenblatt, L. (1969). Towards a transactional theory of reading. *Journal of Reading Behavior, 1*, 31–49.

Rosenblatt, L. (1978). *The reader, the text, the poem*. Carbondale, IL: Southern Illinois University Press.

Rucker, D. (1969). *The Chicago pragmatists*. Minneapolis: University of Minnesota Press.

Sapir, E. (1961). *Culture, language and personality*. Berkeley: University of California Press.

Scheffler, I. (1975). *Reason and teaching*. London: Routledge and Kegan Paul.

Schubert, W. H. (1986). *Curriculum: Perspective, paradigm, and possibility*. New York: Macmillan.

Shumaker, W. (1954). *English autobiography: Its emergence, materials and form*. Berkeley: University of California Press.

Shapiro, S. (1968). The dark continent of literature. *Comparative Literature Studies, 5*, 421–454.

Silverman, K. (1980). *The subject of semiotics*. New York: Oxford University Press.

Smith, S. (1987). *A poetics of women's autobiography: Marginality and the fictions of self-representation*. Bloomington: Indiana University Press.

Spengemann, W. C. (1980). *The forms of autobiography: Episodes in the history of a literary genre*. New Haven: Yale University Press.

Sprinker, M. (1980). Fictions of the self: The end of autobiography. In J. Olney (Ed.), *Autobiography: Essays theoretical and critical* (pp. 321–342). Princeton: Princeton University Press.

Starobinski, J. (1980). The style of autobiography. In J. Olney (Ed.), *Autobiography: Essays theoretical and critical* (pp. 73–83). Princeton: Princeton University Press.

Steedman, C. (1986). *Landscape for a good woman: A study of two lives*. London: Virago Press.

Stodolsky, S. (1988). *The subject matters*. Chicago: University of Chicago Press.

Stone, L. (1972). Prosopography. In F. Gilbert & S. R. Graubard (Eds.), *Historical studies today* (pp. 107–140). New York: W. W. Norton.

Sturrock, J. (1977). The new model autobiographer. *New Literary History, 1*, 51–64.

Tanner, D., & Tanner, L. N. (1981). Emancipation from research: The reconceptualist prescription. In H. A. Giroux, A. N. Penna, & W. F. Pinar (Eds.), *Curriculum and instruction: Alternatives in education* (pp. 382–391). Berkeley: McCutchan.

Thompson, D. (1973). *Discrimination and popular culture.* London: Heinemann.

Tyler, R. (1949). *Basic principles of curriculum and instruction.* Chicago: University of Chicago Press.

Updike, J. (1989). *Self-consciousness.* New York: Alfred A. Knopf.

Van Manen, M. (1990). *Researching lived experience: Human science for an action sensitive pedagogy.* London, Ontario: Althouse Press.

Vygotsky, L. (1962). *Thought and language.* Cambridge: M. I. T. Press.

Walker, D., & Soltis, J. (1986). *Curriculum and aims.* New York: Teachers College Press.

Weintraub, K. J. (1975). Autobiography and historical consciousness. *Critical Inquiry, 1,* 821–848.

Weintraub, K. J. (1978). *The value of the individual: Self and circumstance in autobiography.* Chicago: University of Chicago Press.

White, H. (1978). *Tropics of discourse.* Baltimore: Johns Hopkins University Press.

White, J. P. (1973). *Towards a compulsory curriculum.* London: Routledge and Kegan Paul.

White, M. (1943). *The origin of Dewey's instrumentalism.* New York: Columbia University Press.

Whitehead, F. (1966). *The disappearing dias: The study of the principles and practice of English teaching.* London: Chatto & Windus.

Whitty, G. (1985). *Sociology and school knowledge: Curriculum theory, research and politics.* London: Methuen.

Widdowson, H. G. (1975). *Stylistics and the teaching of literature.* London: Longman.

Willinsky, J. M. (1987). The seldom-spoken roots of the curriculum: Romanticism and the New Literacy. *Curriculum Inquiry, 17*(3), 267–291.

Willinsky, J. M. (Ed.). (1990a). *The educational legacy of Romanticism.* Waterloo, Ontario: Wilfrid Laurier University Press.

Willinsky, J. M. (1990b). *The new literacy: Redefining reading and writing in the schools.* New York: Routledge.

Wimsatt, W. K., & Beardsley, M. C. (1954). *The verbal icon.* Lexington: University of Kentucky Press.

Zendler, B. H. (1960). Dewey's theory of knowledge. In J. Blewett (Ed.), *John Dewey: His thought and influence* (pp. 59–84). New York: Fordham University Press.

About the Author

Robert J. Graham is Assistant Professor of Secondary English/Language Arts Education in the Department of Curriculum: Humanities and Social Sciences at the University of Manitoba, Winnipeg, Manitoba, Canada. He received his undergraduate degree from Glasgow University and holds master's degrees in English Literature from the University of Toronto and in Education from the Ontario Institute for Studies in Education and a doctorate from the University of Calgary. He has published in *Adult Education Quarterly,* the *Canadian Journal of Education, English Quarterly,* the *Journal of Aesthetic Education,* the *Journal of Educational Thought,* the *McGill Journal of Education,* and the *Scottish Literary Journal.* He currently teaches courses in English education, theory and practice of writing instruction, literary theory and English education, and issues in English language arts.

Index

Abbs, P.
  and dialectical pedagogy, 108, 109, 110, 111, 112
  and the politics of teaching, 71, 73, 97
  and the teacher as artist, 100–106, 140
  and teacher preparation courses, 3, 13, 14, 67, 96, 115
Absolutism, and experimentalism, 9, 47–54
From Absolutism to Experimentalism (Dewey), 9, 48
Adams, Henry, 151
Adjustment mythology, 133
Aesthetic theory, 62–63
Affective fallacy, 7–8
Allen, D., 69, 71
Althusser, Louis, 137, 151, 152
"The Analysis of Educational Experience" (Pinar), 121
Antaeus, 41
Anyon, J., 151
Apology, 36, 37
Apple, M. W., 15, 151
Applebee, A., 82
Argument, and cognitive functioning, 61
Aristotle, 60
Arnold, Matthew, 71
Art, and experience, 46, 49, 62–63, 65
Art as Experience (Dewey), 46, 49
Artist
  child as, 95, 150
  teacher as, 100–106, 140
The Arts and Current Tendencies in Education (Britton), 78
Assessment, 87–88
Augustine, Saint, 29, 32, 33, 104, 112
Author
  death of, 19, 147–148

intention of, 36–38
  and the nature of authorship, 22, 145–153
  as painters, 22, 29
Autobiographical impulse, 38–41, 50
Autobiographical pact, 2
Autobiography
  collaborative, 113–117
  contemporary, 143–147
  and definitional issues, 18–26, 32, 37
  and education, 1–3, 53–54, 63–65, 67, 87–91, 101–117
  elements of, 2–3, 23–26, 32, 36, 37
  and epistemology, 3–4, 40, 50, 100
  functions of, 31, 35–36, 153
  ghostwritten, 155–156
  and historians, 26, 29–30, 34, 38, 81
  institutional uses of, 107
  as intervention, 29–30
  limits of, 27–32
  literary, 81, 85, 89, 91, 94, 104
  methodology of, 103–105, 122
  as mode of reading, 7–9, 149, 156
  and point of view, 32–33
  and questions answered, 12, 17–18
  rescuing of, 135–136
  as research method, 99, 113–117
  as scholarly topic, 20
  as self-portrait, 22–26, 29
  struggle concerning, 18–26, 32, 37
  studies of, 20–22
  styles of, 23–24, 34, 36, 37, 39, 40
  subjective aspects of, 107, 142, 144, 149
  validity problems of, 113–114
Autobiorevelatory choices, 40, 112

Ball, S., 69, 72
Barnes, Dorothy and Douglas, 69, 70, 87–91, 93, 94, 138

169